You Can Do It . . . One

"This book will show you how to test-[...]
ing a VocationVacation of your own. [...]
a mentor, how to prepare for the vocati[...]
to do once the vocationing is over. It will map out the small steps you
can take to move from where you are now to where you want to be.

"Along the way you'll meet lots of people who have done it—the
former real estate agent who opened her own clothing boutique,
the former therapist who became an airline pilot, the architect
and air traffic controller who together opened an artisan bread
bakery. You'll hear from them and many others about the fears
and challenges, the mistakes and lucky breaks, and the surprises
and accomplishments they experienced.

"You don't have to be a risk-taker or a Type-A personality to
turn your dream of rewarding work into a reality. All you need is
the desire to change, patience, and a little help from TEST-DRIVE
YOUR DREAM JOB."

—Brian Kurth

Vocationing works! Here's the proof:

"The experience of a lifetime!"
    —Connie Madison, horse trainer vocationer, Roseville, MN

"How do you thank someone who has changed your life for the
better? My winemaker mentorship did just that and opened my
eyes to what the reality of my life can and will be!"
    —Brenda DiMuro, winemaker vocationer, Seattle, WA

"VocationVacations gives our members a chance to test-drive a
vocational interest before they jump in and leave their current job.
It perfectly fits our members' need to investigate and evaluate."
    —Kathi Jones, executive director, Microsoft Alumni Network

more . . .

"Becoming a baker seems doable to me now!"
        —Lea Chadwell, baker vocationer, Winston-Salem, NC

"I have a passion for taking a different look at my life (yes, even at seventy years old!) because of my vocationing experience."
        —Jim Franklin, brewmaster vocationer, Port Townsend, WA

"Thanks to my vocationing experience in 2005, I am pleased to report I have taken the plunge and now work as a full-time professional photographer!"
        —Dan Chaffee, photographer vocationer, Kansas City, MO

"VocationVacations has helped me make the move from being a happy enough international banker to a really, really happy dog trainer. I still can't help but smile when I say that . . . There's just no way I would have had the imagination or the courage to make this shift had it not been for the experience of VocationVacations and the encouragement of the mentors and the career coach I worked with through VocationVacations."
        —David Ryan, dog trainer vocationer, Rye, NH

"After spending two days with my mentor, I decided to pursue my dream job as a concierge. I did it! I've now transitioned from the music industry to the hospitality industry. This is an example of what a VocationVacation can do to help pave the way."
        —Corazon Chacon, hotelier vocationer, New York, NY

"I see the starting point for my dream now and the process necessary to get it going!"   —John Lenzi, restaurateur vocationer, Bronx, NY

"My mentorship was an incredible career-immersion experience. I can think of no better gift for the new graduate, the retiree, or anyone contemplating a midlife career course correction!"
        —Sue Burton Kirdahy, TV producer vocationer, Boston, MA

TEST-DRIVE YOUR
DREAM JOB

A STEP-BY-STEP GUIDE TO FINDING OR CREATING THE WORK YOU LOVE

BRIAN KURTH
WITH ROBIN SIMONS

BUSINESS
PLUS

NEW YORK   BOSTON

Will Wiebe's method, on pages 174–176, has been adapted from "I have something to discern," Personalite et Relations Humaines (PRH) International, 1996, Methodical Personal Formation Program, #6, Copyright 1996 PRH International. Adapted with permission.

Business Plus
Hachette Book Group USA
237 Park Avenue
New York, NY 10017

Visit our Web site at www.HachetteBookGroupUSA.com.

Business Plus is an imprint of Grand Central Publishing. The Business Plus name and logo is a trademark of Hachette Book Group USA, Inc.

Book design by Stratford Publishing Services, a TexTech business

Printed in the United States of America

First Edition: January 2008

10 9 8 7 6 5 4 3 2 1

Library of Congress Cataloging-in-Publication Data

Kurth, Brian.
  Test-drive your dream job : a step-by-step guide to finding and creating the work you love / Brian Kurth. — 1st ed.
     p. cm.
  ISBN-13: 978-0-446-69888-7
  ISBN-10: 0-446-69888-1
  1. Vocational guidance.   2. Career changes.   3. Career development.
4. Vocational interests.   I. Title.

HF5381.K85 2008
650.14—dc22

                                                          2007026003

*To my parents, Harold ("Hub") and Evelyn Kurth,
who inspired us to dream and gave us the love and
encouragement to make those dreams real.*

ACKNOWLEDGMENTS

It has taken the proverbial village to develop this book, the VocationVacations company, and the vocationing process. Sadly, I cannot acknowledge everyone individually. I can, however, thank those who have offered the biggest contributions.

First and foremost, a huge thanks goes out to the VocationVacations mentors all across the United States who prove daily that the vocationing process is viable, powerful, and effective. Mentors lovingly give their time, energy, and commitment to help others take their first step toward changing their lives by exploring their dream jobs. I offer special thanks to Myron Redford at Amity Vineyards in the Willamette Valley of Oregon, who was the very first mentor to sign up with me in 2003, a full six months prior to the company's introduction. Myron saw the vision and trusted this dot-com refugee to pull it off, and is still mentoring today. To the hundreds of other mentors who have followed Myron, I thank you for your passion and commitment to the vocationing process.

To our rapidly growing number of clients ("vocationers"), thank you! "Build VocationVacations and they will come" was my motto when I launched the company as a hobby business in January 2004. And come they did! Special thanks to Gail Haskett for booking the very first VocationVacation in March 2004 (a brewmaster VV for her husband, Steven). Little did she know that *my* dream was coming to life when she booked Steven into *his* dream job experience.

"Build it and they will come," I thought, but I needed people to help me build it. And I found them. Many dedicated, insightful people shared my early vision and pitched in to help me prove that vocationing was an idea whose time had come. In roughly chronological order . . . My thanks go to my friend Berit McClure who wrote the first press release that we sent out to fifteen West Coast newspapers in January 2004 and then worked to create a PR buzz about the company. An enormous thanks goes to Melissa ("Missy") Townsend who came on board in June 2004 "to just help out a bit" and has stayed for three and a half years of unwavering dedication, passion, and hard work. Missy is my confidante, my fellow dreamer and strategist, and, most importantly, my friend. To Kelly Kirkendoll Shafer, my former boss at Ameritech in Chicago, I offer unlimited gratitude for doing an early test-drive VocationVacation, and then piloting the PR efforts that brought the company so much invaluable media attention. I offer limitless thanks to Will Wiebe, who threw caution to the wind when he signed on as VV's first affiliated career and life coach while also managing his own coaching firm. Will has offered endless enthusiasm and moral support to me, the entire VV team, and hundreds of vocationers. I offer huge thanks to Lisa Morgan for coming on board in early 2005 to assist in scouting mentors and building business partnerships. Lisa's ability to "shake the trees" and build relationships is invaluable. I send a big thank-you as well to Hinda Bodinger for her determination and creativity in scouting mentors and helping with business development and academic relations. Hinda was integral to the success of VocationVacations' early days. I am very grateful that Jen Ross picked up a copy of *People* magazine in a hospital waiting room and read an article about VocationVacations. A year and a half later Jen is leading the charge in creating marketing partnerships for the company that inform hundreds of thousands of people about VV and the vocationing process. I hate crunching numbers, which is why I reserve special thanks for Rich Denman, Loree Misch, and John Woolley, who have come on board as financial planning consultants to assist me in business and strategic planning. And I offer special thanks as well to Melinda Ayala-Ford and Sheila Connelly for the guidance and handholding they offer to our customers. In 2007 Dianne Haines so ably took the PR baton from Kelly Shafer. I thank her for continuing to grow our media presence, as well as for the stellar Web content she provides along with fellow writers Erin Abler and Beth Behler.

A round of thanks goes out to our growing corps of affiliated career and life coaches who, in addition to running their own companies, have offered up hours of dedicated and passionate consultation to our clients. In addition to Will Wiebe, Lynn Kindler of Austin, Texas, and Leslie Prager of New York City saw the early vision of VV and helped develop our coaching program. I will forever be grateful to Will, Lynn, Leslie, and all of the VV affiliated coaches for their time, thoughts and wisdom, and for their enormous sense of caring for our clients.

When launching VocationVacations, I knew nothing about television production, but after partnering with Tammy Leech and Russell Best at Brave Street Productions to create a cable network program, I learned a ton! I thank them for their belief in VV as well as their time, effort, and instruction. I also want to thank Al Roker of Al Roker Productions and NBC's *Today Show* for his ongoing mentorship in the world of television production and multimedia.

It is impossible for me to thank all of my family and friends for their nonstop, unwavering support as I worked to fulfill my own dream of creating VV and the vocationing process. This book is dedicated to my loving parents, Harold ("Hub") and Evelyn Kurth. Thanks to Dad for all the pluck and vision you gave me, and for all those times you said, "Son, you know I'm proud of you and what you're creating." Mom, although it has been nearly eighteen years, I feel your loving presence every day and I hear your omnipresent words of encouragement. I also want to thank my sisters Linda Newton and Rhonda Lewis, my brother Terry Kurth, and my eight nieces and nephews for cheering us along. In addition to my wonderful family, I could not have better friends. To Chris Fulton, my coworker in Chicago, I owe a mighty thanks for allowing me to share my vision in her closed-door office back in 1999 during a "what are we doing with our lives?" moment. I thank Mary Lou ("ML") Martino for being a "guinea pig" vocationer in the fashion industry in October 2001, when I had just started playing around with the concept. I thank my ol' college buddy, Charlie Cox, for test driving a brewmaster vocation in Milwaukee, Wisconsin, in January 2002. I give enormous thanks to Gwen Lee Hassan (otherwise known as "Grace" to my "Will") for assisting in pro bono legal work (Okay, the cost of lunch and a bottle of her favorite cologne) to get VocationVacations off the ground and begin the lengthy trademarking process. And I thank my college pals, Anne Martino and Heidi Gutenkunst Wilkinson, for test driving a B&B owner VV together in March 2004, just after our launch.

I have a great working relationship with my literary agent, Susan Golomb. She saw my vision and passion and knew I wanted to share it with others, and took enormous care and time with me at every step of the process. Susan, I hope this book makes you proud. I offer special thanks to Dan Ambrosio and Ben Greenberg, my editors at Grand Central Publishing. English was never my favorite class, but it has been a joy working with you both.

Last, but surely not least, I owe *so* much to my cowriter, Robin Simons. I would never have thought that writing could be fun but Robin made it so. After test driving her own dream job as a horse trainer, Robin immediately "got" the vocationing process, and then, from coffee houses in Portland and Seattle to my family's getaway in Canmore, Alberta, she wrangled me and the book's contents onto the page. Robin has become a true friend and I look forward to collaborating with her again soon. I also have to thank Robin's daughter, Hallie Rosner, for her flexibility and patience while her mom was off writing with me. Hallie, you are your mother's dream and she glows whenever she speaks of you.

All My Best,
Brian Kurth
August 2007

CONTENTS

"The secret of success is making your vocation your vacation."
—*attributed to Mark Twain*

1

VOCATIONING

It started out as a pipe dream. Pure fantasy. It was a notion that popped into my head while I was breathing exhaust on the Kennedy Expressway in Chicago, halfway through my daily twenty-two-mile, one-and-a-half-hour, one-way commute. I didn't think of it as a job or a business; it was simply a wish list—a list of all the jobs I wished I could do instead of the one I was actually doing. It was 1999 and I was thirty-three years old; I was feeling and looking older than my years, gaining weight and losing my hair. With a hard-earned master's degree in international relations, I was spending most of my waking hours plugging numbers into sales and marketing projection spreadsheets for Ameritech, the Midwest's major phone company. *The phone company!* I was a living, breathing Dilbert! It wasn't that I hated my job; I didn't. I had a great boss. I was making great money. In the last decade I had learned a ton about management and business. But in the end, making the world better through broadband technology just didn't set me on fire. Many Friday nights my partner, Doug, and I would get together with friends—two were architects, one was a TV station's programming director, and another was starting his own technology-marketing business. They'd talk about their jobs and their faces would light up. They *loved* what they were doing. Then I'd say something about the latest data network initiative we had launched and in seconds their eyes would glaze over and their heads would hit their spaghetti plates. My job was *boring*. *They* were bored listening to it; *I* was bored doing it!

So every day I spent my commute fantasizing about all the things I'd rather do. Some days I imagined being a dog trainer, walking through the park, a dutiful chocolate Labrador at my side, head cocked to my every command. Other days I saw myself taste-testing wine in a cool, dark cellar in Sonoma County. Still others I saw myself leading groups of tourists through the cobbled streets of Budapest or Buenos Aires interpreting the local culture. With all that fantasy you'd think the commute would have passed quickly—but it didn't. Ninety minutes in Chicago traffic is ninety minutes, no matter where your head is.

One evening I was staring out at the chain of rain-glazed brake lights in front of me, having just called home to tell Doug that, once again, I'd be late for dinner. (As had become my custom, I'd also used a few choice words to describe my commute and my state of mind at that particular moment. To his growing impatience, he was becoming the misplaced recipient of my disillusionment and lack of career fulfillment.) As I clicked off the phone I thought, why am I just fantasizing about these jobs? There must be a company that arranges short-term internships so people like me can try out their dream jobs. That night I went online, but to my surprise I couldn't find one. Nothing on the Web offered the kind of experience I was seeking. Guess I wasn't going to be able to do it after all, I thought. But then a second later I had a brainstorm: if no one else has done it, maybe *I* could do it! I even knew what I would call such a company: VocationVacations, because the company would offer vacations that let you test-drive your dream vocation. And before "reason" could stop me, I registered the domain name: www.vocationvacations.com.

And that was the last serious thought I gave to VocationVacations for almost two years. I was too devoted to making money to think seriously about starting a business—especially one for which there was no precedent. I liked my benefits, I liked my lifestyle, and I liked the nest egg I was building. I liked the security of the life I had created. Sure, my job was boring and I envied friends who loved their work. But it wasn't *that* boring and I didn't envy them so much that I was willing to risk my security for a "great idea." I just wanted to do my *own* little "vocation vacation." I didn't want to create the whole company.

That was over eight years ago. It took me two years, a corporate merger and acquisition, a layoff, September 11, and a stock market "correction" before I realized that working for a corporation was not as secure as I had imagined and I began to take the idea of starting a business seriously. But finally, after I'd left my phone company job, and the "make a million" job I'd taken at a dot-com start-up had imploded, and my hard-earned savings had nose-dived with the stock market, something clicked and I realized there was no point in waiting. Doug and I pulled up stakes and drove cross-country looking for the perfect place to live. Along the way I asked everybody who was standing still if they would want to test their dream job if they had a chance. The answer was a resounding yes!

So I figured I was onto something.

But it still took me a long time to get around to acting on it. We had settled in Portland, Oregon (indifferent to the fact that it was suffering its worst recession in decades), and I wanted to get to know the terrain. My head argued that I better get a job—a real job—and make as much money as I could, but my heart kept me ambling around the city, checking out neighborhoods and coffee-houses, driving down the Oregon coast, touring the pinot noir vineyards of the Willamette Valley, meeting people, and talking about my idea. When reality hit and I realized I needed to make money, instead of looking for another corporate job I went for a dream job of my own—working at a small family wine distributor for a fraction of what I'd been making in Chicago, selling wine out of a white Chevy Tahoe and loving it.

But all the while, VocationVacations was brewing. I asked all the people I met what their dream jobs were, how far they would travel and how much they would pay to try one, and what they would expect in a "dream job vacation." By six months into my wine job I was calling businesses in popular industries, looking for people who were passionate about their jobs and would be genuinely interested in sharing them with others. Four months later, I had ten mentors lined up—in everything from inn keeping and beer brewing to horse training and auto raceway management—who had agreed to take in "vocationers" for one to three days for total-immersion, hands-on learning. Now all I needed was customers. Build it, I told myself, and they will come.

I asked my friend Berit McClure to help me write a press release describing the company and we sent it out to fifteen West Coast newspapers. Nothing happened. Not a single one picked it up. The wine job was starting to look more like a career. And then two months after I sent out the release, *Outside Magazine* saw it and did a story—and everything exploded. The Associated Press picked it up and the next thing I knew VocationVacations was in 250 papers. My home phone (the official VocationVacations telephone) began ringing off the hook, and in March 2004, Gail Haskett bought the very first VocationVacations package—a brewmaster experience at Full Sail Brewing in Hood River, Oregon—as a birthday present for her husband, Steve.

That same month I realized two things: first, if I didn't hustle my buns off and get more than ten mentors I would never be able to meet the demand; and, second, if I didn't grab the momentum while I had it, I might as well kiss the opportunity good-bye. So on March 15, I handed in my resignation at the wine distributor; on April 1, I became the first employee of VocationVacations. I took it as a good sign that it was April Fools' Day.

VOCATIONING: THE FIRST SMALL STEP

Three more April Fools' Days have passed since then—giving me plenty of time to make mistakes, learn on the job, build a fabulous team, feel the fear of being far from shore without a life raft and also the incredible pride and exhilaration that come from knowing you dreamed something and made it happen. In those three years I've watched hundreds of other people take their own first steps toward their dream careers. I've watched an IT programmer test-drive a career in voice-overs and a lawyer roll up her sleeves as a cheese maker. I've cheered as an airline pilot got behind the mic as a sports announcer and a Web designer sat behind the desk in an architect's office. I've watched software engineers put down roots as vintners and a veterinary technician don toque and apron as a pastry chef. People of both genders and all ages, heads of households and single moms, postretirement planners and people just starting out, have all gone starry-eyed into vocationing and come out with something closer to 20/20 vision. And almost every one of them has come away buoyed, invigorated, and more determined than ever to make his or her dream job happen. When I call vocationers six months later, many have actually gone ahead and written business plans, relocated, started school, or in other ways moved their dream job forward. After years of fantasy, something about *living* the job for just a few days empowered them to take action. Partly it was the learning—the concrete knowledge they gained about the desired business. Partly it was the mentor, who held their hand, boosted their confidence, and offered ongoing help. Partly it was the contacts they made, which made taking the next steps easier. But above and beyond those practical things, there was something else: the vocationing awakened and energized something deep inside them. It connected them with the truest part of themselves, a part that had previously felt dormant and that, once awakened, refused to be ignored.

You know—if you're considering a dream job—that the push toward a dream career is not just about how you spend your working hours. It's about meshing your work life with your deepest sense of self. It's about having work that matches your values, that feeds instead of exhausts you, that doesn't require you to leave your priorities at home and check your heart at the door. When we imagine a dream job, we imagine a job in which we are fully ourselves, in which our hearts and minds are equally engaged.

This engagement is what people feel while vocationing. And once they reconnect with that deepest sense of self, few are willing to return to their status quo.

Which of course brings up the next question: what happens *after* vocationing? You go; you fall in love with a career; you leave, fired up to work in your chosen field . . . and then what? Sure, you had a great couple of days; sure, you know what you want to do—but there's a gaping chasm between wanting and making it happen. And when you look down into that chasm it's brimming with house payments, car payments, college educations, health care, food bills, utility bills . . . How exactly do you take the next step?

The question is its own answer. You take the next *step*. The next *small* step. The biggest surprise for people who find or create their dream job is that it doesn't have to happen all at once. It doesn't have to be an all-or-nothing, hold-your-nose leap from security into the unknown. Instead, it can be a series of small steps that you take only as you feel ready. Sure, there are the few really bold (or independently wealthy) vocationers who cut the ties to their previous careers and hurl themselves full-time into new ones. But most people take it more slowly. They continue at their current jobs while transitioning gradually into the dream. They do research, they write a business plan, they figure out how to begin the new career without taking on more risk than they can handle. Some go to school to get more training. Some dedicate a period of time to paying off debt and building savings so they'll have funds for their new careers. Some find work in the new field while they put together a business of their own. The path and the timeline vary from vocationer to vocationer; what they all have in common, though, is the *passion* and the *vision* to move ahead.

Of course, after vocationing, some people find that the job they tried was not the job they thought they wanted. A woman who vocationed with the general manager of a hotel came away exhausted, shocked at the amount of physical energy the job required. Her mentor helpfully brainstormed other hotel-related jobs with her that would involve her financial services background but better suit her "laid-back" manner. A woman who dreamed of being a veterinarian learned while vocationing that while she loved the animals she hated dealing with their owners—and that a better job for her would be working as a veterinary surgeon where she would have minimal owner contact. Finding that you don't love your dream job as much as you'd hoped can be disappointing; the dream is dashed, the "what next?" question is alarmingly reopened. But even people who have that experience usually consider their test-drive a success; they're thankful that it showed them what they didn't want before they ventured further.

For most people—whether or not they find their dream job—vocationing is like opening the door to a long-closed room. Sunlight and fresh air touch something that has long been in the dark, and the result is a renewed sense of self and a new sense of possibility.

So perhaps I should offer a word of caution. Vocationing will be fun (it *is* a vacation, after all); it may be exhausting (people tend to work *hard* at the jobs they love); it will be exhilarating to spend time with someone who works at his or her passion. And it will probably leave you changed. Sandy Huddle put away her dream of doing video production right after college, then years later vocationed in TV production just to "finally close that door." Instead, she came away with her passion so rekindled that within months she had changed locations within her company so she could attend a top-notch school for TV and film production. Robin Simons, who cowrote this book with me, vocationed as a horse trainer "just for fun," not to change vocations; and two days on the ranch so rekindled her childhood love of horses that she's since made time to ride at a nearby stable every day. So don't vocation if you're afraid of sparking something passionate inside you. Do it only if you're ready to be renewed.

YOUR TURN

This book will tell you how to test-drive *your* dream job by creating a VocationVacation of your own. It will tell you how to find a mentor, how to prepare for the vocation, and, most important, what to do once the vocationing is over. It will map out the *small steps* you can take to move from where you are now to where you really want to be. Along the way you'll meet lots of people who have done it—the former teacher who became a country music songwriter, the therapist-turned-airline pilot, the architect and air traffic controller who together opened an artisan bread bakery. You'll hear from them and many others about the fears and challenges, the mistakes and lucky breaks, the surprises and accomplishments they experienced as they moved into their dream careers.

You'll see that few of these people consider themselves risk takers. They describe themselves as "ordinary," "security-oriented," "401(k)-type" folks. Most are still shocked to find they've taken so bold an action. But after years of working in jobs that didn't feed their passions they reached a point when they felt they had no choice: they *had* to push past their fears and make the switch. "I got to the point where I couldn't live with myself if I didn't try," they say. "If I tried and failed, well, at least I'd know I'd tried. Not trying at all would have been failure."

What helped many of these vocationers was realizing that the risks they needed to take were not as overwhelming as the ones they had imagined. The scariest moments—quitting their jobs, purchasing property, signing a bank loan, moving cross-country—didn't occur until they were already far along in their planning, or even until after their new career was already up and running. It was still scary; it was still a risk; but it was a *calculated* risk. By the time they took it, they felt they were likely to succeed.

What if you don't know what your dream job is? What if you're itchy and unsatisfied in your current job but when you think about what's next you draw a total blank? Well, you're not alone. There's very little in our society that encourages us to know what we really want to do. When we're children people ask us what we want to be when we grow up, but once we're teenagers we're taught what we *should* be; we're channeled into a narrow range of careers based on security and stability rather than on passion. The notion that we could follow our hearts when it comes to work is pretty much trained out of us by the time we graduate from high school. So who can blame us if, by the time we realize that our "practical" jobs don't fulfill us, we've already forgotten how to find our own passions inside? That may be another reason to consider vocationing. It enables you to experiment, to test out all sorts of jobs that might be appealing. As Jimmy Jones, a renowned horse trainer, once said, "A man's gotta make at least one bet a day, else he could be walking around lucky and never know it." It's the same thing with dream jobs: you could have a dream job and not even know it if you don't give one or two a try.

KNOWLEDGE IS POWER

Knowing the ins and outs of your dream job—and coming to believe that you really can do it—makes transitioning into it easier. So does knowing other people who have done it. So let me introduce you to three people who left their old jobs to pursue their dreams.

- Sue Burton Kirdahy left her corporate job with no clear idea of where she was headed, then used a series of "experiments" to figure it out.
- Tim Healea *thought* he knew what his dream job was, only to discover through an internship that it was something different.
- Toni Cory had a solid handle on her passion—but no experience to guide her. So she went vocationing to get the knowledge and confidence she needed.

Sue Burton Kirdahy

Sue was thirty-seven and, after fifteen years in financial services market-
ing, was feeling increasingly dissatisfied and unfulfilled in her career. But
as the major breadwinner for her family of four, she was not in a position
to leave. Nor did she know what other path she wanted to pursue. Then a
series of volunteer "experiments" helped her figure that out and opened
the pathway to the career of her dreams.

Right out of college, Sue fell into financial services marketing
and, from the get-go, she loved it. She loved the intellectual
demands, the brokering of big deals, the extensive travel, and
the chesslike challenge of climbing the corporate ladder. But
she also craved creative pursuits—writing, theater, humor—that
had less of an outlet at work, so at night she took classes in those
areas. One class was a course in stand-up comedy. For the class
final, she had to prepare a five-minute stand-up routine and perform it in a comedy club. To her surprise, "the exhilaration and
endorphins I felt coming off that stage were like nothing I had
ever experienced." She had always been "the kid who cracked up
all the others at the bus stop," but she had never imagined that
doing comedy intentionally as an adult would provide so much
pleasure.

Over the next thirteen years Sue thought about that experience
repeatedly, but she never took it any further. "I can't be performing at midnight at some Chinese restaurant and then go into a
big meeting the next morning," she said. But nonetheless, she put
"stand-up comedy" on every résumé. It seemed like an important
part of her identity, and often a hiring manager's reaction was a
good barometer of whether or not she'd fit into that company's
environment.

By the time she was in her thirties, Sue's enthusiasm for her career had begun to wane. She'd gotten married and had children and was cultivating other interests, and while her yearning for creativity was growing, it still had no outlet in the corporate world. Although she was busier than ever—traveling, working sixty hours a week, leading a staff of twenty-five—she began taking more and more classes, even retaking the comedy class she had taken thirteen years before. The mismatch between her "real" self and her work self was becoming starker. In late 2003, in an effort to build its female leadership, Sue's company had her work with a career coach. "As part of the coaching I went through a process to uncover my core values and look at how my life was in or out of line with them. Well, the values I uncovered were creativity, acceptance, and humor, and when I matched that to my day-to-day existence at the company, I was pretty far out of alignment." The misalignment was further highlighted when, as part of a course she was teaching, she wrote a "personal mission statement." Her mission, she wrote, was to "ignite creative transformation in people through the use of humor and play." Not exactly her job description in the corporation. "And once I knew that," she said, "I felt compelled to do something about it." She realized she had to leave.

But how could she leave? Her salary provided 85 percent of the family income as well as the medical benefits. She couldn't just go off and start a business or find a low-paying job in the arts or social services. Hoping for a compromise, she proposed that the company create a new role of "innovation catalyst," which would allow her more creative freedom and positive impact. But, ultimately, the company wasn't able to meet her request. Instead, it asked her to lead an employee engagement campaign that consisted of trying to boost employee morale while strategizing downsizing alternatives and reviewing lists of people who were about to be laid off. It was the antithesis of what she wanted to be doing. So in March 2005 she handed in her resignation. She had managed to negotiate a severance package that would pay her salary and benefits for six more months. That gave her a six-month runway to get a new career—whatever it was—off the ground.

What could that career be? For a businesswoman with an interest in creativity, what kind of jobs were even available? Perhaps TV production? TV producers brought together resources to bring creative ideas to fruition. That might use her expertise and business skills in a new context—but she didn't know the first thing about it. So she reached out to friends, family, and colleagues, asking if anyone knew any producers. Remarkably, several did and she was able to set up informational interviews in order to learn about the field. A friend of a friend was even able to get her an interview with a high-level ABC executive producer who met with her in his New York office. "If you were twenty-two," he said, "I could hire you as my assistant, but you've already had a very successful career and we'll both feel extraordinarily awkward if you're making coffee and dubbing videos." She left discouraged—too old and needing too much money to start over in the world of TV.

Then she learned that she could vocation at Brave Street Productions, a TV production company in New York. Thrilled that she could experience a TV career firsthand, she signed up, and for two days worked with producers Russell Best and Tammy Leech, developing pitch treatments, preparing interviews, editing videotape, reviewing concepts, and setting up location shoots. It was exhilarating and it was exhausting, and by the end of the second day she knew it wasn't the job for her. She had loved the front office work—writing pitches and packaging shows—but she had no interest in the mechanics of production or in being on a shoot. Helpfully, Russ brainstormed other paths she might pursue that would use her business experience and creative talent: perhaps she could be a development executive; perhaps she could package shows and take them to Wall Street to find investors. She was grateful for his suggestions; those were ideas she never would have thought of.

Meanwhile, Sue had begun actively pursuing comedy again. Shortly after she quit her job she had worked up her courage and gone to an "open mike" at a local comedy club. It was terrifying to get up onstage, but, once again, coming off, she felt that endorphin high. In the weeks after that, she had gone to other clubs, met local comics, and begun doing semi-regular stage time. As a result, when Russ suggested that she go to a "boot camp" held by the National Association of TV Program Executives (NATPE) where she would be able to pitch an idea for a program, she knew exactly what she wanted to pitch. Working with the comics she had met, she wrote a pitch for a TV sitcom called *Open Mike,* about the trials and tribulations of a band of small-town comedians. To her surprise, when she presented it at the boot camp, executives from two cable networks asked her to create a demonstration pilot. With further advice from Russ and help from a local cable access director, she and her comedian colleagues taped a ten-minute pilot demonstration. Ultimately the pilot wasn't picked up, but she was thrilled to have experienced the development process first-hand. She'd been out of work for eighteen weeks, she wasn't close to finding a job—but for the first time in a decade she felt she was following her heart and moving ahead under her own creative power.

When there were two months to go before her salary and benefits ran out, she got a surprising phone call. She had made a point of staying in touch with people from her former career, letting them know what she was doing, and now the marketing director at another financial services company called to ask her to help produce TV commercials on a freelance basis; the pay would be close to what she had been previously making. Sue leaped. It wasn't her dream career—the work was about financial services rather than her own creative product—but it was a perfect opportunity to combine her former experience with all that she had learned and it was less than full-time, which would leave her time to continue to explore options. She had started her quest thinking she wanted to be a producer—because that was a title she knew—but her explorations in the world of entertainment were showing her that other possibilities existed. Now she saw that it was only through further "experiments" that she would ultimately find the place that was right for her.

Intrigued by Russ's idea of packaging TV content for Wall Street, she volunteered for a company that found financing for independent films. What she learned was that she absolutely hated asking people for money! She volunteered as an event planner for a children's charity and found that while it was personally fulfilling, it also lacked the creative and intellectual challenge she had been craving. Eventually, her research led her to a motivational humorist named Loretta LaRoche. Loretta's business—using humor to help people manage stress and build resilience—was almost exactly what Sue had outlined for herself when she had written her personal mission statement twenty months before. She had seen Loretta perform and thought her show excellent, so when she learned that Loretta lived in a nearby town, she worked up her courage to call. Her "pitch" was straightforward: "I'm in marketing; I love what you do; maybe there's a way I can use my marketing skills to help you." Over lunch, the two women brainstormed ideas for expanding and marketing Loretta's business; the next week Sue began volunteering, implementing the ideas they had come up with. It was a win-win situation: Loretta profited from Sue's marketing know-how; Sue learned firsthand about life as a motivational humorist.

When they had been working together for several months, Loretta asked Sue to open for her onstage. Sue was terrified. It was one thing to write a few jokes and tell them in a club or bar; it was altogether different to write twenty minutes of inspirational humor and deliver it to an audience of a thousand! It would mean *doing* what she'd said she wanted to do! She wrote a draft skit, tore it up, wrote it again, and then wrote it a third time. She thought it was good—but was it good enough? She performed it for Loretta, who gave her the thumbs-up. Finally it was time to go out onstage. To her amazement, the audience responded. Laughter and applause filled the theater and that endorphin high came back again, even bigger and brighter than it had the first time. When the set was over, Sue knew that she had found not just a career, but a calling.

Today Sue has a "portfolio career," a cluster of part-time jobs all related in some way to her dream career. She works part-time as Loretta's creative director; she opens frequently for Loretta onstage; she also books her own humorous and inspirational speaking engagements. Recently she vocationed a second time with a professional comedian in New York who mentored her on how she could make presenting to corporate audiences a lucrative, full-time career. She still produces TV commercials for the financial services firm to pay the bills, but the old feelings of dissatisfaction and misalignment are gone. "Now I am actually doing what I said I wanted to do two years ago," she says. "I still don't feel as though I've arrived at a final destination, but as time goes on, my transition to my dream career comes more and more into focus. With each experiment I learn more about what I like and what I don't, I make new contacts and learn about new possibilities, and I uncover back-door paths for getting into this career. Maybe most important, with each experiment I live less exclusively in my head and more and more in my heart. I am really enjoying the journey."

Tim Healea

Tim was twenty-three and two years into an editorial job at a New York magazine when he realized that journalism was not the dream career he'd once imagined. But what was? Three internships let him test a hunch and then refine it, and ultimately led him to the job he still adores ten years later.

"I've always been really curious," says Tim. "I love asking questions and exploring new things, so I always thought journalism would be the perfect job." And perhaps it would have been if he had landed a job at a consumer magazine, but right out of journalism school he got a job at a magazine for discount retail chain executives and instead of doing probing interviews he found himself red-penning copy about executive compensation and retail security. Two years in, when he'd been unable to land a more interesting job, he decided that his career in journalism was a failure.

Now what?

He thought about cooking. His mother and grandmother were great cooks and had inspired a similar passion in him. What would a career in cooking look like? Wary after his journalism foray, he decided to do some exploring. School was out of the question—he couldn't quit work to go to school, nor could he do both things simultaneously—so he "apprenticed" himself at a small culinary program in Manhattan. In exchange for helping out in the kitchen, he was permitted to sit in on classes and could do it on weekends and evenings alongside the magazine job.

He loved it. The duties were basic—setting the table, washing pots and pans—but he loved working around food and meet-ing people in the industry. Within weeks he knew it was what he wanted to do. Under the guidance of one of the instructors, who had become both a mentor and friend, Tim decided that instead of spending two years and a lot of money to attend a high-end culinary institute, he would do an eleven-month work-study pro-gram at Peter Kump's New York Cooking School. There he could spend two days working at the school for every day in the class-room, and his tuition would be free. The only hitch would be living money. To attend school, he would have to quit his jour-nalism job; how would he eat and pay his rent? His friend and mentor helped him there as well. Stephen Schmidt was the lead consultant for the new edition of the *Joy of Cooking* and got Tim a part-time job testing recipes. He also referred him as an assistant to Suzen O'Rourke, who ran a private cooking school out of her Manhattan loft. Together, the two jobs would just cover his bills for the duration of school.

Heart in mouth, he handed in his resignation. Standing in his boss's office, for a moment he felt that it seemed crazy to give up the good salary and the stable future publishing offered, espe-cially when he had no idea what he would do when school ended in eleven months. But the minute he left the office and closed the door behind him he knew he'd made the right decision. The *cost* of being in the wrong career far outweighed the security and the paycheck.

School was everything he'd hoped it would be. "I learned as much working at the school as I did in the classroom," he said. "I dealt with all the purveyors and accepted all the deliveries; I devel-oped a close relationship with the instructors; I got a complete behind-the-scenes look at how a professional cooking operation runs." Through his two part-time jobs the learning continued. "Every few days I'd meet with the editor of the *Joy of Cooking*, who was the top cookbook editor in the country. She'd give me a pile of recipes and I'd go home and test them. And at the private cooking school, professional chefs came in to teach and I got to work with and learn from them."

Midway through his course work, Tim bought a book on baking artisan breads. Rustic, handcrafted breads were new in the United States in 1997 and Tim became fascinated. He began experimenting with his own dough and starters and was amazed that with such basic ingredients—flour, water, yeast, and salt—he could create something so alive. When it was time to do an internship for school, he decided to try an artisan bakery and applied to the Pearl Bakery in Portland, Oregon. Unfortunately, Greg Mistell, the bakery's owner at the time, wasn't so sure. He had never had an intern and had to be convinced by one of the managers that taking Tim was a good idea. But within days both Greg and Tim knew they were well matched. "I didn't know going into it that that passion would blossom in me," Tim said. "But when I got there I fell in love with it. Even coming in at four in the morning didn't bother me. I was just so excited to be around bread every day." When the internship ended, the bakery hired him full-time. A year later he became head baker.

For the next four years Tim reveled in the baking. His goal was "to make the best breads and pastries and do the best production work every day"—and he did. In 2002 he was selected to be one of three people on the U.S. team in the Coupe du Monde de la Boulangerie. The world baking competition is the Olympics of the baking profession, and Tim and his team took home the silver medal.

After that, his focus began to change. As much as he loved the baking, he realized he was also interested in learning the numbers side of the business. "It seemed like the natural evolution of my passion," he said. "I wanted to use my creativity and problem-solving ability to look at how to grow the business. I wanted to learn to read a financial statement, how to calculate the break-even point, and how to use numbers to make decisions going forward." So Tim approached the bakery's new owner, Eric Lester, with a proposal for changing his job in a way that would enable him to grow his skills. Eric agreed and together he and Tim developed a long-range plan that would expand Tim's role in the operation.

Today, Tim has moved out of the head baker position into the job of "expert mentor" to the entire bakery staff. "Even a dream job can get boring," he says. "It's not always new and fresh. So you have to take initiative and create pathways so you get what you want out of your life and career." One of his roles today is mentoring other people who want to learn the art and business of baking. It's a full circle that gives him enormous pleasure.

Toni Cory

Toni was forty-nine and facing the closing of the factory where she had worked for over two decades. She knew what she wanted to do next—and it wasn't to take another factory job. She wanted to open her own dog kennel and day care. What she didn't know was how to go about it—until she spent a day with Dawn and Dick Walton at The Dog Zone.

Toni had been working at the Motorola factory in Mt. Pleasant, Iowa, for twenty-seven years when the company announced it was going to close the plant. "I could have found another manufacturing job," she said, "but I was tired of working in a factory. I thought, if it happened here where we're a profit center, it could happen anywhere, and I didn't want to leave one factory and go to another and have it happen again. I was forty-nine years old; I had another twenty years of work. I didn't want anyone else controlling it. I wanted to be happy."

So Toni and her husband, Paul, started planning. Crazy for

their dogs, they'd had dozens of conversations over the years about how much they wanted a great place to leave them when they went away. The conversations had always ended with a little note of fantasy, "What if we started one ourselves . . . ?" Now, suddenly, Toni saw her chance.

As soon as word of the plant closure began to circulate, she took a How to Start Your Own Business course at the community college. By the time she finished, she and Paul had made a plan: they would sell their home and buy a larger piece of property and Paul would take a year off from his one-person construction company and build them a house and a kennel building. Of course, that would require money, which would mean getting a bank loan. So using what she'd learned in her class, Toni wrote a business plan. "I'd never done anything like that in my life," she said, "and I didn't think I could do it. But I'm good at asking for help and my business teacher was happy to give it, and once I got into the zone it just kind of fell out of the computer." To gather the marketing and demographic data she needed she called the local vets. When some were unwilling to give her information, she pretended to be a student gathering data for a paper. When the plan was finished, she put it in a three-ring binder with tabs for every section and proudly gave it to the banker. Although she had been conservative in all of her projections, it showed that the business would make a small profit in the first year.

To her surprise, the banker shook his head. "Toni," he said, "this is rural America. People here think of dogs as livestock. When they leave for the weekend they don't need a kennel. They just throw food down and leave."

But Toni was undaunted. "Marc," she shot back, "whose picture do you have on your desk?"

Marc looked at his desk, where prominently displayed was a picture of his dog. He agreed to lend them the money.

But then he presented another surprise: as a condition of the loan, the bank would require that Toni and Paul put up *all* of their money, even their retirement account. They had expected to use some of their retirement, and had hoped to leave a cushion in the bank for first year operating costs. But the bank was intractable. So after a brief discussion, they agreed. "If we wanted to make our dream come true, this was what we had to do," said Toni. "So we took every single penny of our retirement, plus borrowed one hundred and sixty thousand dollars. Paul even sold the 1970 pickup he'd been restoring for as long as we'd been married. He hadn't been planning to sell it but when you do something like this your priorities change and those things don't mean so much anymore."

So now they had money to build their new home and the day care—but Toni had only the slimmest idea of what was involved in running a kennel and day care business. Nor did she have long to learn. Paul would be taking a year off from his own work to build the buildings, drawing a salary from the bank loan for his time, which meant that when the loan ran out, the business had to be ready to open. So right before her job ended, Toni went to The Dog Zone, a doggy day care in Cedar Rapids, for a day of on-the-job learning. There, Dawn and Dick Walton, the owners, shared everything. "Before I went I could only imagine what it would be like to own a doggy day care, but after spending a day getting body slammed by dogs, pulling rocks from a dog's throat, cleaning the walls, and seeing everything that Dawn and Dick did, the whole thing became real. I left with the confidence that Paul and I could do it."

As soon as her job ended, Toni used her employment benefits to go to the Tom Rose School for dog training in St. Louis to become a certified professional dog trainer. It was an intense five-month program that taught everything from obedience training to the fundamentals of running a dog-training business. Between school and the vocation experience, she was beginning to feel prepared to open the day care. Her excitement and optimism grew when she returned home and saw the progress Paul had made on their little log cabin home and the kennel building. She joined him, diving headfirst into the preparations.

"It was extremely stressful," she said. "In addition to the construction, there were so many things to do and think about: getting signs made, getting the interior done, getting inventory bought, getting the promotional stuff in order . . . And all of it was brand new to me." But with her willingness to ask for advice, Toni found all the help she needed. "There were so many people out there who wanted to help," she said. "The chamber of commerce; my business school teacher; my banker; my accountant; my former neighbor, who was an interior decorator; my vet: I picked their brains for every bit of knowledge I could get and most of the time I couldn't write fast enough to get it all down."

At times a sense of panic would overwhelm her. What are we doing? she would think. We can't do this! When that happened, she and Paul would take a break and drive into town, where inevitably they would meet someone on the street or in a restaurant who would say he couldn't wait for the kennel to open. "That's what really kept us going," Toni said. "We'd say, okay, we're doing the right thing."

Toward the end of construction, the bank money started dwindling. They realized they could no longer afford to pay Paul a salary. And since they had no money left of their own, Toni had to go back to the bank for an additional loan. "When I had to go in and borrow money to live on, I was almost in tears," she said. "Marc said, 'Toni, take a breath. It'll be okay. We'll get through this.' He'd gone from being skeptical to totally believing we were going to make it. Once he started talking to people and saw how

I DON'T KNOW WHAT MY DREAM JOB IS!

It sounds silly since I'm in the dream job business, but when I was thinking of leaving my "heads in the spaghetti plates job" at Ameritech, I didn't know what *my* dream job was either. That was one of the reasons it took me so long to quit. I didn't know what I wanted to do instead. It got to the point where even I couldn't stand my own whining. Then one day I got an idea. I bought an enormous piece of paper and $100 worth of magazines and newspapers and got on a train to Springfield, Illinois. I had no particular interest in the Land of Lincoln; it was the downtime I wanted—eight hours on the train with no phone, no TV, nothing from real life demanding my attention. I spent the time doing what I hadn't done since kindergarten, cutting out pictures that appealed to me and pasting them onto the paper. When I was done, I had a giant collage of travel, animals, food, buildings, fitness, and the arts. I sat back and examined it almost as if another person had done it. It was a portrait of *me*: all the pictures were of things that gave me pleasure, things I wanted in life, things that in some ways defined me to myself. The next day the train pulled back into Chicago and I folded the collage and tucked it in my suitcase. It hadn't told me what kind of job I wanted, but it had opened a door. It had reminded me that there were things in the world I loved and that any one of those areas would provide a job with greater meaning.

Eventually I found work that incorporated almost every one of them.

Doing a collage is just one way of getting in touch with passions deep inside you. Another way might be doing online searches based on your avocational interests, or "going back to school" by reviewing college catalogs for signs of interests that have gone dormant. Perhaps it would be helpful to talk to people who knew you as a child and might remember things that sparked your passion then. Numerous books and Web sites can help you pinpoint your interests as well as possible careers.

excited people were about it, he started saying, 'Toni, people will pay for this! You have to charge more!'" The bank was quick to approve an additional loan.

Finally the building was done, the signs were in place, the details were taken care of. In early October 2006 Toni sent an e-mail to her former colleagues at Motorola inviting them to her grand opening. It was almost exactly a year to the day since she had left her job.

That October Toni took in $670; in November her receipts were $2,600. People who weeks before didn't know what doggy day care was were bringing their dogs to try it out, falling in love, and becoming regular clients. Strictly word-of-mouth marketing was attracting customers from as much as an hour away.

Today, the business is seven months old and receipts continue to grow. Toni is working harder than she expected to. "I probably put in eighty hours a week," she says. "I'm here from six in the morning to seven-thirty or eight at night, and Paul comes in at night to help with cleaning," but she expects in a few months to hire part-time employees. By the end of the first year, she expects the business to support her.

"This has definitely been the experience of a lifetime," she said. "At times I wondered whether we would live through it emotionally, financially, and physically, but Paul and I have really jumped out of our boxes on this and I am really proud of us."

WHY SPEND TIME VOCATIONING?

1. To "test-drive" your dream job before committing
2. To find a mentor
3. To learn the "ins and outs" of the business
4. To make contacts in the industry
5. To boost your confidence
6. To explore a passion
7. To satisfy your curiosity about "the road not taken"
8. To test possible careers when you don't know what's next
9. To experience an unusual, invigorating vacation
10. To try something new and challenge yourself in new ways
11. To gain perspective on your current job, lifestyle, and future
12. To reconnect with a dormant part of yourself

How Can You Be Inspired and
Immobilized at the Very Same Time?

If I had read about Sue, Tim, and Toni eight years ago when I first had the idea for VocationVacations, I would have thought, well, good for them, but I can't do that; not now, maybe not ever. As much as I wanted to, the idea of leaping out of my "real" job and trying to start my dream job just seemed too ambitious. I was inspired—but I was also immobilized. I was impassioned by my idea—but too scared to do anything about it.

Perhaps that's how you're feeling now. I know that what I needed more than anything then was help getting past my fear. I needed someone to tell me that:

1. going after my dream job *didn't* require the daredevil leap that I thought it did;
2. what it did require was a series of small, incremental steps; and
3. those steps could be fun rather than scary.

If someone had told me these things back then I might have been skeptical—but I also might have been willing to give it a try. Instead of hanging on to my various cubicle jobs for so long, I might have started VocationVacations six years sooner.

You are probably skeptical too. The idea of giving up the security of a "real" job—with a real paycheck and real benefits—is pretty scary no matter how you cut it, and imagining even the most exciting dream job doesn't do much to mitigate that fear. The only way to do *that* is to address those fears head-on. So let's do that right now—because the sooner you get mobilized, step by incremental step, the sooner you'll make that dream job real.

2

FEER

Let me tell you a story about immobilizing fear. My own.

In December 1991 I graduated from Loyola University in Chicago with a master's degree in international relations and big dreams to see the world. So when I heard about a professor in Estonia (*Estonia?*) who wanted help starting a retail office automation business with some of his former students, I could hardly get my résumé off fast enough. The Berlin Wall had come down just a couple of years earlier, the Soviet Union was imploding, the Baltic nations were in the process of splitting off and regaining their independence; it was a historical moment and I wanted to be there! Apparently, the fact that my retail experience was limited to a stint at the May Company right after college was not an impediment, because I was hired and a month later I found myself on a boat crossing the Baltic Sea from Helsinki, Finland, to the beautiful Estonian capital, Tallinn. When halfway across I found myself wondering why I had committed myself to spending an undetermined period of time in a place where the Russians had just cut off the oil supply and I didn't speak the language, I reminded myself that eighteen months before, my mother had dropped dead of a heart attack while ironing and that two of my first cousins had died before they turned thirty-five. You only live once, I thought, and I was not about to spend my life avoiding adventure and playing it safe.

Unfortunately, three months later, somewhere over the Atlantic on my trip back home, that fear-be-damned attitude dropped away. I got back to Chicago flat broke (even in Estonia my salary in Russian rubles hadn't gone far) and took a job at Saks Fifth Avenue, where I'd worked part-time during grad school, so I could make some money while I looked for a job in international relations. Now, perhaps you're thinking Chicago is not exactly the hub of international relations. Of course, you're right. But I was too "broke" (I told myself) to move to New York or Washington, DC, where the prospects would be better. In truth, I was too scared. Estonia had been a lark—short-term, with a secure job and my expenses paid. But New York or DC with no job and barely a friend—those were scary! So I spent months pursuing jobs that weren't there, until finally I gave up and took a job at AT&T.

And you know the rest. Enter Brian the conversation stopper. Brian, the heads-in-the-spaghetti-plates bore. So did I leave? No! Did I remember that little lesson from my mom and cousins? No! Did I say, "Hey, Brian, you just spent several months in Estonia, for crying out loud; you can blow this pop stand and find yourself something closer to your dreams"? No! I hung in there. I wanted the money. I wanted the security. I was too scared to go out on my own.

So from 1993 to 2001 I stayed in telecom—where I worked hard, learned a ton, had wonderful bosses who truly were my mentors—and yet felt as if I had sold my soul. As Doug said, it was "LAN WAN, thank you, ma'am"—a whole lot of activity with zero heartfelt connection. I felt like a captive in the land of diminishing returns: the more I put out, the less satisfaction I received. And then, in late 2000, I was handed a golden opportunity to pursue my dream job: Ameritech, the company I'd switched to, was acquired by SBC and my entire department was let go with pretty handsome severance packages. All except me. *I got offered a promotion.* But what did I do? Did I say, "Thanks but no thanks, I'm following my heart"? Did I say, "Sorry, but I know an exit opportunity when I see one"? No! I took it! As if somehow, with a new company and a new title, broadband telephony would suddenly fill me with a sense of purpose. I lasted six weeks—*and then I blew my chance again!* When it became clear that to keep my job I'd need to move to Texas, I quit— but did I stop to figure out what I really wanted to do? Did I act on that fabulous idea I'd had sitting in traffic, the business I'd named and even bought the domain name for? No! Even before I quit, I lined up another job!

This time, of course, I had good reason. I went to work at a dot-com start-up. You know how much money they were making in 2000. It was the height of the bubble; everyone and his brother were raking in the dough. How could I pass that by? Sure, the company managed Internet security, not the world's most scintil-lating product. But I figured five years, then I'll cash out with a million in my pocket and I can do whatever I please! Why would I turn that down?

Maybe because people just a little more savvy than I were already seeing the writing on the wall. Sixteen months later we were all laid off. The dot-com bubble had burst.

The morning we got the announcement I called Doug, then cleared out my desk and tried to conjure an ounce of sadness— but I couldn't. All I could think was, no more commute! I'm free!

Five hours later I was sitting at home—my initial euphoria starting to look more and more like panic—when the telephone rang. It was Doug, calling from *his* dot-com job.

"You sitting down?" he asked. After six years together it was easy to hear the anxiety in his voice. "I'm getting laid off, too."

For a fleeting moment the panic threatened to consume me,

but then, just as quickly, it turned into something else. *Finally!* I could barely stop myself from laughing. Finally, even *I*, cautious and fearful as I was, couldn't miss the message. The universe was doing what I'd been unable to do for myself: giving me the corporate boot. "Okay, Brian," some cosmic voice was saying, "you get one more chance. And this time, see if you can get it right!"

> "I 'outed' myself. I told everybody that I was leaving financial services and looking for work in TV production and stand-up comedy so that when I got scared and wanted to back down I would be too embarrassed."
>
> Sue Burton Kirdahy, who left a career in financial services marketing to create a "portfolio career" including comedy, motivational speaking, and video production

What followed was a period of bliss. For the first time I decided to do what I'd been too scared to do before: take some time to think about the future. And what I thought about was Vocation-Vacations. Why *couldn't* I do it? Between my savings and the money I pocketed each month from a rental apartment in Chicago, I had enough money to live on for a while *and* to start a business. I would be crazy not to do it! So when Doug's company offered him the chance to try a lateral move to a position at their headquarters in Calgary, Alberta, we barely thought twice. He had possible job security and I figured I could launch the business from there. It felt like a brand-new chapter.

We arrived in Calgary on September 10, 2001.

In the wake of September 11 all of my excitement turned to fear. The stock market had plummeted and suddenly instead of being an entrepreneur with a great idea and a year's worth of cash, I was an unemployed dreamer with three mortgages and two-thirds

DREAM JOB CLUB

Behavioral economists, who look at how people make choices, are well aware of the fact that we tend to choose the thing that feels most desirable in the present and postpone a harder or riskier choice until the future. Fortunately, they've also noted ways that people work around that. One solution is to *precommit,* that is, to take an action that requires you to make that more difficult choice *now.* An example is a Christmas club at a bank: customers commit to paying a certain amount every month so that, come December, they'll have their gift money ready. Precommitment is also an excellent strategy for circumventing fear. When Sandy Huddle said to the VV office, "Let's book it now because once I've done it I can't talk myself out of it," she was precommitting herself to something that felt scary. That way, when the time came, if her brain's limbic system urged her to put off the vocation, she would no longer have the option.

Throughout the dream job process there are many ways you can precommit to circumvent your fear: schedule a vocation three months in the future because that far away it won't seem so scary; register for school now even though it won't start until the fall (same reason); commit to a bank loan or a lease or a business partner even if those actions scare you silly.

Don't commit if on every level you question the decision, but *do* commit if in your heart you know your course is right and it's only fear that is making you waffle.

the investments I'd had before. *What had I been thinking? We had to go back to Chicago and get high-paying corporate jobs!* But even then, with the world shaking under my feet, I knew I couldn't do that. Maybe it was having lost so much money so precipitously through no fault of my own. Maybe it was the realization, as my mother's death had been, that life can wallop you while you're busy making plans. Maybe having already reached the point where I'd decided to do VocationVacations I was too far gone to turn around. For whatever reason, I suddenly got it: *I had nothing to lose!* If I tried VocationVacations and it failed, I could always get another job. *This* was my time. I needed to do it *now*.

So Doug and I sold the condo in Chicago and used the money to finance our drive across the country. It was on that trip that I began to research VocationVacations, and in Portland, Oregon, our new home, that I finally worked up the courage to get it off the ground.

In the years since I started VocationVacations I've talked to many people who gave up "security" to start their dream jobs, and I've discovered that most people had an experience similar to mine. They spent *years* thinking about making the switch before finally taking action. Like me, they had found their fear insurmountable. They'd had a million reasons for not doing it: kids in school, mortgages and tuitions to pay, an impending promotion, not the right time . . . Every reason was completely legitimate, but somehow, at a certain point, those reasons ceased to matter. Sometimes the reasons actually went away (the kids graduated, the mortgage got paid off), but just as often the underlying situations didn't change. What changed was something inside the people. They had crossed a line. They had moved from a place where they were making *rational* arguments for not pursing their dream to making an

BE ANGRY. BE VERY ANGRY.
DO NOT BE AFRAID.

Ordinarily, people are not encouraged to be angry, but when it comes to dream-job seeking, anger can serve a very useful purpose. According to decision scientist Jennifer Lerner, anger makes people more optimistic and less risk averse. Lerner's specialty is studying how anger shapes our view of life and influences our decisions. In one experiment she showed research subjects an anger-inducing photo of Arabs celebrating the 9/11 attacks and showed others a fear-inducing photo of postal workers wearing masks to protect against bioterrorism. The subjects who saw the anger-inducing photo were much more likely to downplay the future risk of both terrorism and personal misfortune than those who saw the fear-inducing photo. Lerner notes that anger has also been linked with stress-induced ailments such as heart disease, but suggests that short-term anger in response to a specific situation may be different from the kind of chronic anger that has been implicated in the other studies (*Pittsburgh Post-Gazette*, The Thinkers, "Emotions' Effect on Decisions Is Her Field," March 28, 2005).

So if one of the things that is pushing you toward your dream job is anger at your current situation, perhaps it's not all bad.

emotional choice to do so. And once that line was crossed, there was no turning back.

So what is it that gets us to that line? If you, too, are wishing for your dream job but are immobilized with fear, how can you get to that line yourself? Let's take a moment to look at your nemesis, fear.

When it comes to fear, we are little better than rats. Brain research shows that we are wired to choose instant gratification over long-term gain. Much as we want our dream jobs, our brain's circuitry pushes us to stay with the secure jobs we already have. "There's a fundamental tension, in humans and other animals, between seizing available rewards in the present, and being patient for rewards in the future," says behavioral economist David Laibson. "If you ask people, 'Which do you want right now, fruit or chocolate?' they say, 'Chocolate!' But if you ask, 'Which one a week from now?' they will say, 'Fruit.' *Now* we want chocolate, cigarettes, and a trashy movie. In the *future* we want to eat fruit, to quit smoking, and to watch Bergman films" (*Harvard Magazine,* "The Marketplace of Perceptions," May-June 2006). In other words, *now* we want our steady paycheck and benefits; in the *future* we'll risk pursuing the job of our dreams.

What causes us to favor the immediate over the long term? It isn't simply impulsivity. It's caused by the interplay between our brain's limbic and analytic systems. The limbic system, the seat of our feelings, controls our emotional response to situations. It functions a bit like an impatient child: strenuous, demanding, and wanting immediate gratification. The analytic system, on the other hand, controls our thoughts, and more closely resembles an experienced lawyer, staying cool and rational even under stress. Whereas the limbic system places a premium on rewards in the present (it wants what it wants *now*), the analytic system values future rewards just as highly. Research subjects, for example, who were offered a choice between taking $20 now or $23 in a month usually chose the smaller amount now because the limbic system was activated by the option of an immediate payoff. When the subjects were offered $20 in two weeks or $23 in a month, however, most took the larger amount because when the payoff was entirely in the future, the limbic system became less active and the analytic system was able to accept the better deal.

Apply this to leaving our current jobs and pursuing dream jobs and you can see how, in a sense, our brains are wired against us. Our analytic systems can do a stellar job acknowledging the long-term bennies that come from working jobs we love, but our volatile, protect-me-now limbic systems start to hyperventilate at the idea of losing the secure jobs we have now. No wonder we have a hard time getting past our fear!

And as if our own physiology weren't obstacle enough, there are plenty of other factors that encourage us to stay where we are. Money, family, loss of identity, fear of exposing the "real you," the "fraud factor" (that voice in our heads that says "you mean you really think you can *succeed* at that??") are all steely-gripped forces that work to keep us where we are.

But they don't *always* keep us where we are. Despite the fact that everyone faces those hurdles, some people manage to surmount them and move forward toward their dreams. People with nothing in the bank quit their jobs and open successful businesses. Sole earners with families to support move cross-country to work at starting wages in their career of choice. People who have spent years building respect and credentials in their profession chuck it all and go back to square one in another. And people who are terrified to expose the dream they've sheltered inside for decades manage to give up the career that was "expected" and take up the very different kind of work they love. How do they do it? What enables them to put aside their fear and take the risk?

FEAR FIGHTERS

Often when I describe the process of dream job seeking, people will say, "Well, I couldn't do that because I'm not the right kind of person," as if there were a certain personality type that is capable of making the switch. I know what they mean. They have the idea that the type of person who can successfully pursue a dream job is someone who is exceptionally gutsy (or perhaps foolhardy); is very decisive and assertive; has a high tolerance for risk and ambiguity;

> "Fear is like a veil. You can choose to stand behind it or you can choose to walk through it. If you walk through it you'll learn something. I couldn't let my own fear paralyze me."
>
> *Sandy Huddle, transitioning from the insurance industry to video production*

and has a history of creating opportunities and trying new things. I suppose if I hadn't seen so many different types of people successfully create their dream jobs, I would assume the same thing, but I've met enough vocationers to know that isn't so. Successful vocationers seem to come in all personality configurations: some are so assertive they resemble bulldogs, while others seem so timid you wonder how they're able to ask for water in a restaurant. Some have a history of starting new ventures and others have worked entire careers in the same job. Some rattle off decisions with the force of a pile driver; others deliberate until the last possible moment—and then change their minds! Whatever you imagine the right personality type to be, I am sure I can find you a successful vocationer who turns your stereotype on its head.

But that's not to say that successful dream job seekers don't have anything in common. They do. The more vocationers I talk to, the more I see certain *attitudes* that most of them share. Regardless of their proclivity toward risk or their level of assertiveness, they have similar ways of thinking about life and themselves that make it easier for them to proceed.

1. *A clear vision.* Successful vocationers tend to have a clear image of what they want to do. It may be a particular job ("I want to be a talent agent with my own agency"), it may

be a type of work ("I don't know if it's singing, dancing, or acting; I just see myself performing in front of a camera and onstage"), it may be a lifestyle and a location ("I want to work outside in a warm, sunny climate"). Though the level of specificity and detail varies with the vocationer, what they share is a clear mental picture of themselves doing that kind of work. The clarity of the image acts like a magnet pulling them forward. When they meet obstacles along the way, that magnetic image rallies them and keeps them moving toward it.

2. *Optimism.* In addition to having a clear vision, successful vocationers *believe* that their vision will pan out. Other-wise, they wouldn't do it! Some have a general confidence in their own abilities based on a history of success; others believe that this particular venture is primed to succeed. They know that failure is possible (and occasionally can't stop that fear from creeping in) but most of the time they anticipate success as if that were the far more likely option.

3. *Comfort with failure.* When they do consider failure they don't become terrified. Their attitude is "What's the worst that can happen? Whatever it is, we'll deal with it." They imagine a period of difficulty and adjustment after the fail-ure, and then life moving forward positively once again.

4. *A high self-standard.* Over and over, in different words, I hear successful vocationers express the same sentiment: "I would rather try and fail than know I didn't try." "I don't want to grow old and wonder 'what if I'd tried?'" "I would be so disappointed in myself later if I hadn't given it a try." It is a recurring theme: what pushes them past the fear is the knowledge that by *not* trying they will be letting them-selves down.

Not everyone who makes the switch has every one of these factors, but the people who successfully undertake dream careers seem to have most of them. Together, these attitudes make a package that seems to make it easier for people to move out of their comfort zone and try something new.

But even these attributes don't fully explain why some people switch and others don't. Something is still missing from the equation. And that missing something, I believe, is *timing*. People who make the switch have reached a point in their lives at which they simply have no choice. It is no longer a matter of wanting to make a change. They *have* to.

When the Pain of Staying Put Outweighs the Fear of Making a Change

I'm the perfect example. How many years did I stay with a job for which I really had no passion? How many exit opportunities did I pass up before I finally took the hint? It took me so long because all those years, unhappy as I was, *my fear was greater than my unhappiness*. But then suddenly something switched. Was it the sudden loss of my dot-com job that led me to question my once comfortable illusion of corporate security? Was it the fact that Doug got notified of his layoff on the very same day (which I, of course, took as a cosmic sign)? Was it simply that I had reached the point at which I lost respect for myself, that the Brian who was so afraid to take the risk was simply not the Brian I wanted to be? Most likely it was a combination of the three. But some constellation of events pushed me over the line to a point where the unhappiness-fear equation inverted; to a place where *my unhappiness became greater than my fear*. And in that moment my desire—no, my need—to pursue my dream became unshakable. Not even 9/11 and my losses in the stock market could deter me.

WHEN IS IT TIME TO LEAVE?

According to business writer Seth Godin, most people stay in their jobs too long. They stay for many reasons—familiarity, inertia, fear of change, attachment to coworkers, reluctance to lose their salary and benefits—but there's a danger in overstaying. In a 2006 column on Monster.com, Godin cautions that by staying too long we hit a personal plateau in which we stop growing. "Look at if from the point of view of evolution," he says. "The species that evolve the fastest are the ones that don't mate for life. By continually reshuffling the gene pool, [they] create something new." The same is true at work: by challenging ourselves to step out into the new, we increase our capacity to grow.

Another argument for pursuing a dream job.

This is exactly what I've heard from most of the vocationers I've spoken to. Do you remember Tim Healea in Chapter 1? Despite the financial insecurity he knew was coming, he felt he had no choice about leaving his work in journalism to go to cooking school because "the *cost* of being in the wrong career far outweighed the security and the paycheck." Sue Burton Kirdahy said essentially the same thing: "I felt like someone had put me in a corner and closed off all the exits. I wanted out but I was stuck. Until finally it got so bad that I was more *unhappy* than I was stuck. Then the decision to leave was almost easy." Said another way: eventually the pain of *not* acting outweighs our fear of making a change. It simply becomes too uncomfortable to stay. That is the point at which we accept the risk of change.

And that is a magic moment—because the moment we cross that line, things that previously felt like insurmountable fears begin to look more like manageable hurdles. Now, on your way to work you find yourself dreaming up ways to overcome them. Instead of wishing there were a way that you could move forward with the dream, you find yourself thinking about *how* you're going to do it. Instead of imagining some vague, open-ended timeline, you start fixing your actions to concrete dates when you know you will be able to act. An enormous internal shift has taken place, and now even such major fears as money, family, identity, and exposing the "real you" begin to lose their insurmountable quality. As if a locomotive has begun rolling inside you, from that moment on, you steadily gather momentum.

MONEY FEARS

For many—maybe most—people this is the big one. There are bills to pay, kids and parents to support, health care to think about, retirement to save for . . . You can't just pick up and pursue a dream that's financially insecure. The total impracticality of that is reason enough to stick to your commute even as you spin dream job fantasies in your mind. Certainly that was my biggest issue. I had money in the stock market that could have supported me for several years, but I didn't want to risk it. The conservative Midwesterner in me had an absolute horror of financial insecurity and that fear paralyzed me for a decade. It wasn't until I passed the unhappiness-fear inversion point that I could act despite the fear.

* * *

Jim Pierce had a similar need for financial security—and found a different way past the hurdle. He had worked in human resources for thirteen years when his company was bought out and its operations moved to Sweden. Then he had to decide: did he want to look for a similar job with a different company or did he, at the age of fifty-one, want to pursue his real passion—working with horses? He'd become enamored with horses a few years earlier and he had found that he had a particular knack for the difficult and sometimes dangerous job of horseshoeing. Compared to the desk-bound, often politically charged work he was used to doing, the idea of being a full-time farrier, horse dentist, and trainer had a certain appeal. "Horses are a little more direct than a lot of the people I'd been working with," he said. "If a horse intends to stand still and let me work on his feet he lets me know, and if he doesn't, he lets me know that too." But with a family to support, and retirement to think about, how could Jim suddenly become a horseshoer? The training, tools, and travel were expensive; the income would be minimal, at least to start; there would be no benefits. It was financially inconceivable!

His wife was the one who talked him into it.

Tonya was working for an industrial linen supply company, where she wasn't terribly happy. *Her* dream was to be a veterinarian, but that required too much schooling. Becoming a farrier, however, would require only three months of training, so she proposed that they go to horseshoeing school together. Jim balked. It was too impractical, too risky. They didn't have money for the tuition (let alone travel to Michigan, where the school was located, and subsistence costs while they were in school). They would have even less money when they came back. And they shared custody of Tonya's two teenage children. It was too big a financial risk.

"But it's only money," Tonya argued. "What's the worst that could happen if this doesn't work? We'll go out and get other jobs."

"She is a real positive influence on me," says Jim. "I'm the one who goes, 'yeah, but' and 'what if?' but her attitude is 'Are we going to die? If not, let's do it!'" So, persuaded by Tonya's optimism, Jim agreed.

But that still left the matter of money: they needed several thousand dollars for tuition, plus money to live on for three months while attending school. And since they had no way of knowing how long it would take for the horseshoeing business to support them, they needed money to live on once they returned home to Washington State. There was only one way they could possibly get the funds: cash out their 401(k)s. *Cash out the 401(k)s?* The very thought made Jim's stomach tighten. It ran counter to every fiscally conservative bone in his body. But now something else was at play as well: the vision he held of the two of them as farriers. He could picture them driving from one ranch to the next, setting out their tools, talking with the owners who would become their regular clients, feeling the horses' breaths and weight against their backs as they worked. He saw them owning their own time, doing what they loved, and that vision—with its powerful emotional charge—was even stronger than his fear of losing his retirement. It made him willing to take the gamble. It wasn't a first choice—his heart still raced at the idea—but now that they had pointed themselves toward their dream, it seemed a necessary and acceptable option.

Two months later, cash in hand, they drove from Washington State to Michigan to attend the three-month horseshoeing program. There, classes in horse anatomy and physiology, working metal in a forge, and lots of practice on horses from nearby stables confirmed that, from a passion standpoint at least, they had made the right choice. What was less obvious was that horseshoeing would support them. But on their last day in Michigan, a chance encounter at a campground offered what they could take only as a sign. Jim was packing their truck to leave when he struck up a conversation with a fellow resident of the Boy Scout camp where they'd been staying. "I've got a couple of horses that need shoeing," the man said when he heard that they were farriers. So before they even left Michigan, they got their first paying job.

Jim has been shoeing now for four years. The first year was tough. He and Tonya drove circles through a three-county area, stopping at every house where they saw a horse pasture and handing out their card, but they had few clients and during the winter when things got slow, Jim went to work as a security guard to make ends meet. They wondered how long they'd be able to do it. By the end of the first year business had improved slightly, but not enough to pay all the bills, especially their expensive health insurance premium, so Tonya took a full-time position with a title insurance company where she would get benefits. She continues to shoe on weekends for pleasure. But in the years that followed the business continued to grow. Jim's clients consistently recommended him to others, and within three years of starting, simply through word of mouth, he found that he had as much business as he could handle. He no longer had to take "the horses with lightning in their eyes and the clients whose checks didn't always clear the bank."

Do he and Tonya have less money now than they would have if he'd taken another human resources job? No doubt. Jim's not earning as much as he did before and has not replenished his retirement account. (Thanks to her job, Tonya is rebuilding hers.) But does he ever regret his decision? Not for a minute. "We took a really big gamble," he says. "It was hard to step out on faith and do this. But I'm really glad we did. I'm the only one from my class who is still a full-time, practicing farrier, and I feel good about that—that I've been able to stick with it and make it work. There were sure times when I thought I better start looking at the want ads! But at the end of the day you feel like you put in a good day's work, like you earned your keep, and I sure do like that."

For Jim, becoming emotionally wedded to his dream job enabled him to move past his fear of financial insecurity and to finance his dream by cashing in his 401(k). Other people have found other ways to finance their transitions to a dream career:

- Haneefa Malik sold her home and moved in with her mother so she would have money to go to fashion design school.
- George Kelley and Paul Holje opened a bakery together, in part so that one could keep his day job while the other worked full-time at the business.
- Andrew Mason negotiated with his company to let him tele-commute three-quarters time so that he could move from Seattle to Oregon to purchase a house with enough land to plant a small vineyard.
- Dan Nainan transferred within his company so he could move from California to New York in order to pursue a career in stand-up comedy.
- Dan Chaffee continued to work full-time while building his photography business on the side.
- Tim Healea and Sue Burton Kirdahy, whom you met in Chapter 1, got part-time jobs in their dream fields to support their transitions to their dream careers.

Most of these people would tell you that they never imagined themselves making the kinds of accommodations they made in order to finance their dreams. But once they passed the point where the pain of staying outweighed their fear of moving forward, they became more willing—*and* more creative. At that point they began to see ways to make the dream come true.

FAMILY FEARS

Jim Pierce was lucky: his wife shared his dream. For many part-nered people it's not so simple. Family or relationship constraints sometimes make it hard or impossible to pursue a dream career. There may be children or a spouse who want to stay where they are while your dream job requires moving to a different location; there may be parents who require your support, leaving you no time, money, or energy for a new venture; there may be a part-ner who is unwilling to take the financial risk, or close family members who don't support your desire for change. Some of these obstacles may be truly intractable; however, others might be surmountable with a little patience and creativity. Sometimes postponing the dream for a calculated period gives you time to do the necessary research and planning. When Cyndi and Mason Cobb decided they wanted to run a bed-and-breakfast, they were unable to move because their daughter had three years left in high school. They used the time to do extensive research, plan-ning, and vocationing so that when their daughter graduated, they were set to go. Sometimes revising your dream plan brings it into the realm of the doable. Mark Spoto had planned to open his own coffeehouse, but the risk involved made his wife nervous. To assuage her fears he decided, instead, to buy a franchise, with the idea that he would introduce his own personalized elements once the business was on firm footing. Sometimes simply moving ahead shows the family how serious you are about your dream and helps break down their objections. Hilary Cooper-Kenny, who was transitioning from nursing to becoming a full-time weaver, fell in love with an old house that she desperately wanted for her studio. When her husband objected (it cost too much, required too much work, and they were supposed to be downsizing) she agonized for four days before making a deposit on it herself and telling her husband, "I was a single mom for a long time, there were many things I passed up because I couldn't afford them or the time wasn't right. This time, my heart is telling me I have to do this. For one time in my life, I have to do something for me." It wasn't easy doing something that her husband so adamantly disagreed with, but Hilary could visualize the renovated house and the impact it would have on her budding business and she simply knew it would work out. What's the worst that can happen? she thought; they'll take the house back. But she knew she'd work extra nursing shifts rather than let that happen. A year later, when much of the renovation work was done and it was time to paint the outside of the two-hundred-year-old colonial-style house, Hilary's husband objected to her plan to paint the white clapboards yellow. "You can't do that! It's disrespectful of the house!" he said. "Who loves the house now?" Hilary chided, and he had to concede that he did.

Hilary was lucky; the conflict between her marriage and her dream was fairly easily resolved. For others, though, the conflict may be more intractable. The process of pursuing a dream job awakens our deepest sense of self, and sometimes that self fits less than comfortably into our existing relationships. Some vocationers, newly awakened, find that they want more from a relationship than they had been getting—or that they want a different kind of relationship from the one they have. They feel like a new person in an old suit in which the waist and shoulders no longer fit. Not surprisingly, tension arises. Sometimes that tension is resolvable. Through therapy and conversation the vocationer and his or her partner may be able to change the relationship so that the "new self" has room to flourish and the partner, too, has room to grow.

Sometimes, however, the partnership is inflexible and breaks under the strain. I speak from experience. Despite all my effort to deny it, one of the biggest obstacles to *my* dream turned out to be the person I lived with.

I guess you could say our conflict began before we even left Chicago. Although I didn't realize it at the time, Doug and I had different visions for our lives. Once I "got" that I needed to pursue VocationVacations, I also realized I needed to leave Chicago: Doug and I were jobless, we were ready for something new, there was no reason to stay. Doug, however, was more cautious. "What if we can't find jobs?" "What if we exhaust our savings?" He was less unhappy with his previous life, and therefore, perhaps, less deter-

GETTING PERSONAL

In his book *What Should I Do With My Life?* Po Bronson says that no matter how dissatisfied we are in our jobs, we don't tend to leave until the discomfort "gets personal." That is, feeling unchallenged or undervalued, or even feeling that your work has no purpose, will push you to *think* about leaving, but you won't actually make a move until something happens that strikes a potent emotional chord. He tells the story of a successful investment banker who had become increasingly disturbed by ethical compromises he felt he was being asked to make for his job. But although he argued and dragged his feet, he could not bring himself to quit. One day the banker came home from one of his regular, week-long business trips, eager to see and hold his baby son, and to his chagrin, his son cried when he walked into the room. To the baby, he had become a stranger. At that moment he knew he had to leave.

mined to create something new. Ultimately, however, he agreed and we made the move to Portland. Once we got there, though, the trouble began again. Because I had made the lion's share of the money in Chicago, we had agreed that Doug would now be an equal, if not the principal, wage earner so that I could start VocationVacations. To do that, he would take a higher-paying corporate job instead of working as he usually did in academia. But Doug didn't want to leave academia and as a result he dragged his feet. When he did finally get a job, it didn't pay enough to support us both, so I needed to honor my end of the agreement and work as well. That's when I took the job with the wine distributor. I didn't really mind working that job—I'd always wondered what it would be like to work in the wine industry—but I was angry. I'd covered more than 50 percent for many years; this was supposed to be my time to start my company.

Over our first year in Portland the tension between us mounted. Doug wasn't happy and partly blamed me for making him move from Chicago, and while I was thrilled to be in Portland, I couldn't get over feeling gypped. Finally the tension got so thick that we couldn't stand it. We had two choices: go to therapy or call it quits. We chose therapy. The therapy was helpful—we improved our communication and talked through several issues—and five months later we felt solid enough to buy a house. Three weeks after closing on the house, Doug moved out. The relationship was over.

I spent the next few months devastated, paralyzed with grief and fear. Not only was I now without my partner and best friend of eight years, but I was in a new city, starting a brand-new kind of business, with no real idea of what I was supposed to do. I sold the house at a slight loss and rented an apartment just so I'd be in a new place of my own. From my bedroom window I could see Mount St. Helens, and every morning I'd lie in bed and look at the mountain. You blew your top in 1980 but you're still here, I'd think, and now you're rebuilding. It gave me a bit of solace—and enough courage to get out of bed and start the day. Then I would pour myself some coffee and pour *myself* into VocationVacations. VV became my therapy. It was the thing that organized and gave meaning to my life. In between sales calls to wine retailers for my wine distribution job, I'd stop in and introduce myself to prospective mentors; at home at night I'd write up mentoring contracts; on weekends I wrote content for the Web site. I worked at a fevered pace—and as the company came together I realized that my "fever" wasn't just because I was sublimating my grief and fear in the business; it was because now that Doug was gone I was able to do what I had somehow felt constrained from doing all along. While Doug had never outwardly disapproved of VocationVacations or done anything to hold me back, he hadn't fully supported my efforts. His work inclinations were simply more conservative than mine; he would never have done such a thing himself, and I think on some level, my doing it made him uncomfortable. He had said to me once that he was holding me back from my dreams, and at the time I had pooh-poohed him. But now I saw that he was right. As painful as the breakup was, I had to admit that if we had stayed together I might never have started VocationVacations.

Nor might I have developed myself fully. Once I was out of the relationship, not only did I fast-forward VocationVacations, but I fast-forwarded myself. I lost thirty pounds, got in shape, and through reading, hiking, and meditation reexamined my own needs, values, and desires. In the process of losing Doug I reconnected with my body, mind, and soul.

Today, when vocationers occasionally confide in me that they feel a conflict between their spouse or partner and their dream job, I can't tell them what to do or what is right. All I can do is ask these questions: What does the deepest part of you desire? Does your partner understand just how important this is to you? How can you be truest to yourself?

IDENTITY

How many years have you been in your job?

How many years have you spent acquiring expertise, earning the respect of colleagues, forging contacts, gaining confidence, building the self-esteem that comes from doing a job well—in short, creating an identity based on your job? Why would you want to give that up? Especially to face a steeplechase of beginner's hurdles? No wonder we resist pursuing our dream jobs. It challenges our sense of who we are.

Until one day that sense itself becomes uncomfortable. One day the self we have become at work clashes so strenuously with the self we feel inside that we start to feel we are living a nine-to-five lie. That's the point at which we start to take our dream jobs seriously.

That's what happened for Carolyn Walker. Carolyn had been a lawyer for fourteen years when she began to chafe at her job. "There were some aspects of the practice that I really enjoyed," she said, "but when I was younger I loved making jewelry and beading and doing crafts projects, and I lost track of that creative side of myself while I was busy practicing law." Still, it took her another several years before she was able to act on her dissatisfaction. Why? It wasn't the money, which she had enough of. It wasn't family, since she was single and unencumbered. "It was the identity," she said. "I was well respected in the firm and the legal community. I knew what I was doing. I felt like there wasn't any challenge I couldn't handle. For years I had worried, even after I made partner, what if I do this wrong, what if I give this person the wrong advice or fail to make the proper argument? But I had gotten to the point where I felt really confident in my abilities. I wasn't *satisfied,* but I was very comfortable, and that made it hard to leave."

Ironically, that was also what pushed her on her way. After years of thinking about leaving but not acting, she reached a point where the comfort itself became uncomfortable. "I felt, okay, I've done this and I could continue to do this forever. And that wasn't comfortable either. To think that this was what I would do for the rest of my life was not appealing to me at all." The Carolyn she was seeing herself become was not the Carolyn she wanted to be.

As often happens, her mounting discomfort made her open to finding an "out." When she made the acquaintance of a woman who had started an upscale knitwear business and needed a business partner, Carolyn quit the law firm, signed on as partner, and invested in the company. The women initially worked well together and Carolyn, who had no background in business, learned a tremendous amount. But by the end of two years, it had become clear that the business would not support them. They felt they had no choice but to try to sell it.

In the meantime, however, working in the fashion business had reignited Carolyn's creative juices. She had begun beading and making jewelry once again, but this time, instead of assembling ready-made materials, she found herself wanting to design and create pieces herself. She wanted to learn to work in gold and silver. So, as she began to disengage from the knitwear business, she made two decisions. The first was to take jewelry making seriously, to pursue it as a career and not just a hobby. The second was to get the best hands-on education she could so she would be well equipped to go out on her own.

Carolyn contacted a local jeweler whose work she admired to ask his advice about pursuing her education. To her surprise, he offered to take her on as an apprentice. So she began going to his studio several days a week, helping out where needed in exchange for learning jewelry making and design. At the same time, she enrolled in metalsmithing classes where she learned to work gold and silver into the shapes she was designing.

Today Carolyn is engaged in the gradual transition from knitwear to jewelry. Because she is committed to her knitwear company until they sell it, her jewelry time is limited. She can produce only enough pieces to sell at home shows, through the occasional event booth, and through private orders. But already, that level of sales is generating buzz and income. Cathy Waterman, a well-known jewelry designer, praised her work and introduced her to the owner of Twist, a store that features some of the finest jewelry artists in the country. She plans, once the knitwear business is behind her, to pursue large wholesale orders from stores such as Saks and Barneys, which, she believes, will provide income enough to support her. It's an ambitious plan but, given her reception and success so far, seems justified.

So for the moment, Carolyn is between identities—no longer a lawyer, not yet fully a jewelry designer. She is operating without a professional identity, the thing she most feared losing. And how is that for her? Surprisingly, it is fine—because she finds that being a novice in a field she loves is thrilling. "I have so much to learn," she says, "and I love learning it. I'm doing exactly what I want to be doing." Bit by bit, she is building her new dream identity.

THE "REAL ME"

Here is one of the cruelest ironies of pursuing a dream job. On the one hand, we feel compelled to find our dream job because our current work doesn't mesh with our truest self, but at the same time the idea of pursuing that work can be paralyzing. What if I pursue the "real me" and then I don't like it? What if I show the "real me" to the world and other people don't approve? What if the "real me" wants things that don't fit with the life I'm currently living? Or, scariest of all, what if I pursue the "real me" and then I fail? Much as we yearn internally to be our truest selves, exposing that self and acting on its wishes can feel like opening a giant can of worms.

Sandy Huddle had dreamed of going into TV production for as long as she could remember. She majored in it in college but was forced to drop out and go to work when her father suddenly died. Although she always planned to go back, she got caught up in the work world, moving up the ladder in the insurance business, conforming to what she felt the corporate world wanted her to be. The creative Sandy who had drawn and photographed and played guitar got buried deeper and deeper. In 1996 when she was thirty-two her company moved her from Pennsylvania to upstate New York. The move proved pivotal. Something in the relocation helped her see how much of herself she had given up. *What happened to you, Sandy?* she thought. *You've abandoned every part of you that was creative.* She began taking guitar lessons again for the first time in fifteen years, and as if the music had unlocked a buried treasure chest, other interests exploded out. She began journaling and writing stories again; she revived her love of theater and began attending Broadway and community productions; and gradually, over a five-year period, she began to think about finding a different kind of work, work in which she could be creative. But what? And how? The unknown answers to those questions kept her from acting.

One day she was talking with a friend who was lamenting her own career

> "I thought, how will I live with myself if I don't do this?"
>
> *Sandy Huddle, transitioning from the insurance industry to video production*

dissatisfaction and the many reasons she couldn't change direction, and Sandy heard herself say, "Your problem is you just don't want to give anything up to get there. It's the 'yeah, but' syndrome: 'yeah, but I'll have to work different hours; yeah, but I have credit card bills.' Well, you pay off your bills. And your job isn't the end-all job; if you really want to do something else you can give it up. It's just easier to say you don't know what you want to do than to take responsibility for what you have to do to get there." She was shocked at her own words. That night she said to herself, "You can't wait any longer to do this. You want a more creative job? Then take responsibility for yourself! What are you going to do to get there?" She decided she had to pay off her credit card debt so that if she had to take a lower-paying job she could still make ends meet. And she decided that she couldn't stay in upstate New York; she needed to move closer to New York City, where there would be more opportunities in the arts.

Almost immediately she requested—and received—a transfer to her company's Philadelphia office. As she was moving she came across her college yearbook. When she saw her major, video production, her reaction was visceral—a mix of disappointment, wonder (*could she still . . . ?*), and fear: she couldn't possibly go back to that! It was way too late, it was far too scary. Immediately, she closed the book. A month later she heard about VocationVacations. Could they possibly have TV production? The idea of reopening that dream was too frightening to pursue: what if she did and then lost it again? She did nothing with the information. But the thought haunted her and a few weeks later she went to the VV Web site, scrolled around, and saw it: a VocationVacation at Brave Street Productions in Manhattan. Instantly she turned off the computer. Butterflies seemed to be flying around behind her heart. She wanted desperately to do it but knew that the days when she could make a career in TV production were long past, and the idea of tasting and then losing the dream again was way too painful. But something inside her wouldn't let it go. Nervously, she called the VV office. "Do you want to book it?" asked Melissa Townsend, who is in charge of mentor relations. "No!" Sandy answered, "I'm not ready." But a second later she changed her mind. "Let's book it now," she blurted, "because once I've done it I can't talk myself out of it."

Remarkably, once she booked the vocation, her fear vanished. She navigated the trains to New York, registered at a hotel, toured the city, and even took in two Broadway shows as if she'd been doing such things all her life. It wasn't until she showed up at Brave Street that the fear returned. She was met at the door by a young man right out of college and saw immediately that everyone else in the studio was ten to twenty years her junior. They were where she would have been if she had never moved into the corporate world. I can't do this, she thought, I'm way too old! The tremendous sense of loss returned. Fortunately, Russell Best and Tammy Leech, Brave Street's owners and her mentors, were closer to her age and made her feel at home and she spent the day fully embroiled in multiple aspects of TV production. But that night Sandy went back to her hotel room and bawled. The reconnection and the loss of her dream felt like too much to bear.

The next morning Russ asked how her first day had gone. "I went back to the hotel and cried," Sandy told him, and explained why. "Your age is not a problem, Sandy," Russ told her. "I know a woman who went back to school in her forties and now she's working in TV production here in New York City. The kids here are great, but you bring other skills to the table." Sandy looked at him in disbelief. "Sandy," Russ said. "It's never too late to be who you might have been." It was a quote from George Eliot and it became Sandy's mantra.

The vocation changed everything. "I thought it was going to

put a period at the end of the sentence," Sandy said, "but it didn't. It blew everything wide open." When she moved to Philadelphia she had moved in temporarily with her mother and stepfather while waiting for her house to sell; now she decided to stay with her folks and save the house money for school. She looked into schools with excellent video production departments and enrolled at the Art Institute of Philadelphia because it would enable her to keep working. She wanted to put away as much money as she could because she knew she would need it when she finished school. Then she went to her boss and, with tears in her eyes, explained her journey and the importance of school, and asked her to approve a schedule change that would accommodate her classes. Within two days—uncharacteristically fast—the company approved the new schedule.

Sandy is now in school and loving it, and is thrilled with herself for having made the choices she made. Remarkably, all the fear is gone. "It's amazing," she said. "I look back at myself three years ago and so much has changed about my life and me. That fear that was so stifling is gone. I still don't know what will happen in the future. At some point I'll have to give up my job. How will I pay for health insurance and car insurance? Will I be able to get a job where I make enough to cover those bills? Right now I'm just looking at getting through school; I'll deal with that stuff at the other end. But I resolved a long time ago that for me it's not about the money, it's about happiness, and this is making me happy."

GETTING PAST THE FEAR

For Sandy it was fear of reopening and then losing her dream, for Carolyn it was fear of losing her identity as a capable attorney, for Jim it was fear of financial insecurity. In truth, there are a million reasons why you can't do your dream job! But they are all *rational* reasons. And when push comes to shove—or when fear of moving comes up against the pain of standing still—the decision to go after your dream job is *emotional*. All the rational reasons in the world roll over and show their bellies once you've reached the point where you simply have to act. So how do you get to that point? Ah! If there were a clear path it wouldn't be emotional, would it? You could read a book, do the steps, and voilà! But it *is* emotional, which means it happens differently for everyone. Talking to people who have done it helps: they prove it can be done. Vocationing is a big help: it's a painless way to build your confidence and excitement. But *the single biggest thing you can do to get yourself past your fear is to look at that fear head-on.* Because fear is like a swiftly moving cloud that is always right behind us. No matter how fast we run, it is always at our back. But if we stop and turn around, the cloud keeps moving. It barrels right along, filling us with strong emotion, and then moves on—and we are left standing in clear air. From that moment on those fears will seem less overwhelming.

So if fear of moving is paralyzing you, *examine* your fear. Figure out exactly what it is you're most afraid of. Are you afraid of losing all your money? Play that fear out to its most irrational, exaggerated end. Will you lose your house? Have to move in with relatives? Land on the street? Will you be unable to afford health care when you or your loved ones get sick? Will you be ill and penniless when you grow old?

Often, a general, undefined fear, or a surface fear, masks a deeper fear about our very survival, which in the dark of our unconscious has grown out of proportion. Fear about losing money, for instance, may be, at the deepest level, a fear that we literally won't survive. When we bring those deepest fears to light and examine them with reason, two things happen: first, the fear shrinks back to something more realistic (you see that of course you will survive, this is really just about money, and although money and survival may feel interconnected they are actually two separate issues); and, two, you can address the realistic fear about losing money with rational plans. Suppose you do lose all your money? How will you handle the situation? Perhaps you'll move in with relatives for a while. Eventually you'll get a new job. Your job will offer benefits, easing your fears about health care. Hopefully your worst-case scenario will never come to pass, but simply thinking through it will do a lot to ease your fears.

> "I had to get over thinking, I used to be a big corporate player and now I'm just sloshing coffee. That was hard. I did a catering job for a fraternity at Yale, my alma mater. Before that, I'd only returned to recruit for my company and people had sort of kowtowed to me. But now they were offhandedly saying, 'Just put the coffee over there,' and had no idea who I was. Emotionally, it was a blow. But it also told me I had put way too much emphasis on how my job related to my position in society, and that I had tied up way too much of my personality and self-worth in my work if something as banal as that could crush my ego."
>
> *Duncan Goodall, owner, Koffee, in New Haven, Connecticut*

Perhaps your fears are not about money, but about family. Are you afraid of angering your partner? Of letting your family down? Of letting *yourself* down if you fail? Whatever your fears, play each one out to its most irrational end: perhaps your loved ones will lose respect for you; perhaps they will leave you, perhaps you'll end up (once again) old, sick, and alone. Let yourself feel the deep emotion associated with each of those scenarios. Yes, it may be painful for several minutes—but once the strong emotion passes you will see rationally that there is a way past each of those calamities. You will have eased the grip that those fears have over your life and made it easier to move forward.

Talking about our fears also helps minimize their power. Often we unintentionally strengthen our fears by holding them inside where they grow and fester in the dark. If we talk about them we expose them to the air—and to another person's perspective. That helps us see them in a more rational, less exaggerated light.

Another way to minimize fear is to use an "exposure hierarchy," that is, to expose yourself to the thing you are afraid of in tiny increments so that you build your tolerance over time. Just as someone who is afraid of driving would be taught to drive in tiny steps—first simply sitting in the driver's seat, the next day turning the car on without moving, days later stepping on the gas and inching forward—you can use the same step-by-step approach to overcome the fear of moving from current job to dream job. The first small step is vocationing. It's fun, it's risk free; it's like driving without the hazards. Once vocationing increases your comfort level, you can move on to the next step—perhaps a second vocation, perhaps further researching your dream career, perhaps taking a course in how to start a business. The move from current job to dream job can be broken into as many small steps as you like, and spread over any period of time. The key is that you need never move on to the next until your own impulse drives you to do so.

FEAR REDUX

I wish I could tell you that once you conquer your fear you need never face it again, but, alas, it isn't so. Fear is pretty tenacious. It comes back and back and back, ferreting out every nook and cranny of the dream job–seeking process to raise its gnarly little head. After a bout of negative self-talk ("Oh, come *on*, you know you can't *really* leave your job") you work up your courage and make the decision to try vocationing—and then, wham, right away you have to work up your courage *again* to call prospective mentors ("What if she laughs at me? What if she hangs up the phone?"). Once the mentor agrees and you have your vocation scheduled, bam, fear shows up again when it's time to report to work ("What if they don't like me? What if I make a fool of myself?"). Unfortunately, the harsh truth of the matter is that fear is apt to be an intermittent companion throughout this process. But that's the key word: *intermittent*. It will come, and go, and each time it comes you will manage it. And gradually you will see that you have a track record of overcoming fear. At that point your own fear may become less fearsome. You may even begin to recognize each new fear as a milestone, because with each new fear you're further down the road, edging closer and closer to your dream.

3

RESEARCH

After we both lost our jobs, Doug and I had three weeks in Calgary while he tested out a permanent job opportunity at his company's headquarters. I decided to use that time to research VocationVacations. I was sold on the idea—I couldn't imagine that people offered a chance to test-drive their dream jobs would turn it down. (Even if you never made the switch, who would pass up a chance to live a dream?) But I had enough common sense to know that I couldn't assume that the rest of the world would feel the same way. I also knew I needed to research something more fundamental: the very notion of the test-drive itself. Would people who were already working jobs they loved be willing to share their expertise with others? What if they saw it as training the competition? Or as simply a time-consuming distraction? Of course, I would pay them an honorarium, but that wouldn't fully compensate them for the time they spent away from their real jobs, training total strangers. Maybe my whole vision was one of those head-slapper great ideas *in concept* that, put to the test, would be a total dud. I had to find out. So when I could tear myself away from CNN and the deteriorating state of the post 9/11 world, I scrolled around online, learning as much as

I could about the "dream careers" that stoked the fantasies of my friends—wine making, horse training, fashion designing, cooking—and casually looked for people who might be "mentors" to people interested in switching careers.

After three weeks in Calgary, Doug and I decided that, beautiful as it was, Calgary was not the place for us; we needed to go back to Chicago, pack up the condo (which we had already sold), and hit the road. That gave me two months in the Chicago area to test-drive the idea of the test-drive. I pulled out the phone book. Because one thing I wanted to try myself was dog training, that's what I looked for: a dog trainer who would be willing to take me in for a day and show me the tricks of the trade. The first three I talked to blew me off. I could practically hear them thinking, What? You think there aren't enough of us in this city already? You think, just for fun, we should give ourselves a little competition? You expect us to let you interact with our customers' dogs—as if our insurance premiums aren't high enough already? I was deflating faster than a poked balloon when the fourth one *got* it. She got totally jazzed about communicating her knowledge to someone who shared her passion. The part of me that had already written off VocationVacations as a failure did a whirlwind 360. *How could I ever have doubted? It would be a total winner!* So later that week I spent two days as a dog trainer. I had a blast and my mentor seemed to enjoy it as much as I did. She soaked up all my questions, told me more than I could possibly digest, laughed at my mistakes, and told me how much she appreciated "giving back" because of all the people who had helped her along the way. By the time I left, I was like a dog with a new bone. Not only did I know more about dog training than I had ever expected, but I was pretty certain that my idea for VocationVacations was viable.

But one-person research does not a business make. I needed to do more test-drives. I needed to know if they would work for people other than me. So I set up two more dream job experiences: one for my thirty-eight-year-old friend Charlie, who had fantasies of being a brewmaster, and one for my fifty-eight-year-old friend MaryLou, who was in the process of separating from her husband and needed something to take her mind off her distress. Charlie went off to a microbrewery in Milwaukee (the Chicago microbrewery never returned my calls), where he had a fabulous time observing every step in the brewing process; MaryLou spent a day with the fashion coordinator for Saks Fifth Avenue, Chicago, where she had a ball. (Their personalities couldn't have been more different; I think sweet, conservative MaryLou was a bit awed at first by Saks's high-powered, high-heeled fashion guru, but they totally hit it off.) When the two vocations were over I could already envision the article in the *Wall Street Journal*: "New Company, VocationVacations, Creates a Niche and Fills It." With all the hubris of the novice entrepreneur, I had no doubt the company would succeed.

When I could pull myself down from my cloud, however, I had to acknowledge that my *Wall Street Journal* welcome was a bit premature: I still needed to do more research. The concept worked—mentors *would* come forward; people *could* go and have a fabulous time working in their dream careers—but what careers did people want? Would they be willing to pay to do this? Would they be willing to pay enough for me to cover expenses and make a profit? I needed something that resembled market research and at least a back-of-the-envelope estimate of costs and income before I filed my corporate papers. So as soon as the house was all packed, Doug and I hit the road. The plan was to take six months driving cross-country looking for the perfect place to live, and I planned to use the trip to further research VocationVacations in every location we visited.

And that's what I did. Everywhere we stopped I asked people

what their dream jobs were, if they would pay to test them, and how much they would be willing to pay. By the time we settled in Portland, Oregon, I had a long list of dream careers, a sense of how much I could charge, and how many I would need to book each month to make a viable business. The research and the numbers suggested I could do it. I had what I needed to start creating the business.

INSIDE OUT

I was able to start my research on the "outside"—researching the market and the viability of my idea—because I already knew what I wanted to do. But for some people, the research needs to start on the *inside*. Those people know they want a change but are not sure what direction they want to go; they may not even be entirely sure of who they are and what they really want. They need *internal* research.

Joanne Bruner is the perfect example. At the age of fifty-nine, Joanne decided that she wanted to own a bed-and-breakfast. The process that led to that decision began with an *aha* at her fortieth high school reunion. Joanne had spent years raising her family, following her husband as his career shuttled him around the country, leaving friends behind in each location, and always putting herself last. But it was at the reunion that she suddenly felt the magnitude of her loss. There, in the embrace of old friends, she realized how much she missed the stability and intimate camaraderie that come from spending years in the same location, and how much control she had given up in her life. She came away from the reunion determined to stop moving, put down roots, and find work of her own. But how?

When she got home from the reunion Joanne began doing an

internal inventory. What were her strong points? What gave her pleasure? What did she need in her life to make her happy? She knew she was a "people person" who loved to entertain, and that she was willing to have a long-distance marriage, if necessary, to remain in one location. Briefly, she revisited the idea of running a tavern, something she and her husband had considered years before—but when she looked at it practically, it seemed too demanding: in order to succeed financially the tavern would need to be open 360 days a year. That wouldn't give her the flexibility she wanted. Then she hit on the idea of a bed-and-breakfast. A B&B was a lot like a tavern—she could "entertain" by providing food and interacting with others—but she could also close it seasonally to allow her to rest and travel.

The more she thought about it, the more the idea of a B&B

WHAT TYPE ARE YOU?

As you consider your dream job options, consider taking a personality assessment. Assessment instruments such as the Myers-Briggs Type Inventory are designed to help us better understand our own behavior and attitudes. They can help us understand why we make the choices we do, how we interact with others, and the types of work and work environments for which we are best suited. The assessment instruments are usually a set of questions for you to answer; many can be done online with the results displayed immediately. The Myers-Briggs (MBTI) is the most well-known assessment but there are many others as well. If you do a Web search for "personality assessments" you will find several. Many sites offer a short free assessment with a more comprehensive test available for a fee.

felt right: it meshed with the strengths and needs she'd uncovered during her inventory; it was something she could imagine herself doing. She was ready to move on to the next phase and start learning about the world of inn keeping.

DREAM JOB 101

It's one thing to think you want to run a B&B, however, and another thing to know if you can really pull it off. As any innkeeper will tell you, the art is in making it look easy. Did Joanne have any idea of what was really involved in running an inn? How much effort it would take? How much staff? How much money to purchase an inn and keep it going? Did she know how much she could expect to earn, or what kinds of problems to expect, or what kind of support is available to innkeepers? No. She knew virtually nothing. She needed a crash course in B&B basics. She got it, first and foremost, by going online.

The Internet is the researcher's best friend. Almost everything you need to know to get up to speed on your dream career is available online. All it takes is a little creativity and persistence. A Google search for "bed-and-breakfast business," for example, brings up a ton of information about starting and running a B&B. On just the first page alone there are six links to advice on starting a B&B, four to B&B-specific business plans, three to B&Bs for sale, two to the Web sites of specific B&Bs, one on how to create ambience in a B&B, and one selling an online room reservation system. Some of these links are to companies eager to sell you their products or services, but almost half are to organizations that provide free assistance. Who knew so much info was available so easily! Search "B&B industry" on Google and you'll find links to the B&B and Country Inn Marketplace, which has links to innkeeper discussion forums, innkeeper associations and newsletters, and seminars for aspiring innkeepers; a link to the B&B page at About.com where an article by a B&B owner details the pitfalls of running an inn; and a link to bedand breakfast.com which has lists of B&Bs across the country (contacts!), info about the industry, and networking and resource material for innkeepers, including a page called "Is Innkeeping For Me?" which offers numerous resources for aspiring innkeepers. Just by using these two Google pages you can get the equivalent of a 101-level course in B&B operation.

That same wealth of information is available for any dream job you might search.

PERSON TO PERSON

The Internet is the place to start your research, but it's not the place to finish. If you use only the Web, you'll end up with stacks and stacks of printed material and a decent theoretical knowledge of the industry but there will be a lot you won't learn. You won't learn much about the pragmatic, human side of the business. What are the people like who work in that field? What has their experience been? How is this career as a lifestyle? How much do they *really* spend and earn? How long did it *really* take them to be up and running? (Those figures may be different from what you read online.) Unfortunately, unless you're incredibly gregarious and fearless, contacting real people is harder than just sitting in your house and scrolling, especially if you feel as if you're asking a favor. But person-to-person research will give you a much more accurate picture of your dream field.

How do you contact complete strangers and tell them you want to learn about their field?

1. Start by making a list of questions you want to ask them. (See the box on page 70.) You won't get to ask all those questions in a single phone call, e-mail, or visit, but listing them will help you organize your thoughts.
2. Prioritize the questions. You want to ask your most important questions first; you don't know how long you'll get to talk.
3. Go back to your research and pick out five or six people you're going to contact. It doesn't matter who or where they are; they can be people who are doing exactly what you want to do, or simply people who are knowledgeable about the industry, and they can be in your hometown or across the country. Ultimately you'll reach out to many more; these are just to get you started. Having a target five or six will ensure that you don't quit if the first one is unresponsive.
4. Phone or e-mail? Both. Make your first contact by e-mail: it's more respectful of your research prospect's time. Tell the person why you're writing, what questions you're hoping to ask, and ask if there's a time when she could spare fifteen minutes to talk. If she's willing, ask her to give you several times when it would be good for you to call. That way, when you do get her on the phone, you'll know you've got her attention.

   If a prospect doesn't get back to you after a few days, send a second e-mail. Perhaps she meant to reply but got sidetracked. If your second e-mail gets no reply, let it go and move on to your next contact. You *will* find people who are happy to help you. It may take ten e-mails to find one, but every field has people who are passionate about their work and love sharing it with others. Keep the faith, be persistent, and you will be rewarded—not only by the information you receive, but by the sense of excitement

QUESTIONS TO ASK

Your research at this stage does not need to be exhaustive. You'll be doing more research with your mentor and even more after your vocation. Right now you just want to get a basic 101-level education in your prospective field. Here are some things you'll want to know:

Lifestyle

- What is the typical lifestyle of people in this field?
- Are there opportunities where I currently live or would I have to move?

Finances

- What kind of money do people tend to make in this field—initially and after several years?
- What kind of investment is necessary to get into the field?

Education

- What kind of education or training do people need to succeed in this field? Are there exceptions?

The Industry

- What are the current trends in the industry? Is it expanding? Shrinking? Saturated?
- Where are the new opportunities in the field?
- What are the biggest challenges facing businesses in this field?
- What is the success rate of businesses in this field?

This is just a starter batch of questions; you'll think of many more as you do your research. Later, when you work with a mentor you'll get a chance to ask much more personal questions: What has *your* experience been? How do you think this applies to *me*? After your vocation you'll focus on *how* to move into your dream career. But this is your chance to sit back and just immerse yourself in your dream. There's nothing you *have* to do right now except have fun learning.

you will feel when you make that connection with someone in your dream field.

5. Once you have someone on the phone, be sure to ask your contact who *else* you should talk to. Who else does she know who might be helpful to you?

You will be surprised at how fast the contacts and ideas build up. Each contact will lead to others and will suggest ideas you hadn't thought of, and soon your desk will be cluttered with notes and folders. It won't be long before the phone calls become easy, your questions become more targeted, and you find yourself actually enjoying the process.

FRIENDS OF FRIENDS

In addition to talking to people you *don't* know, you also need to talk to people you *do* know—and sometimes that is even harder. It can be challenging to tell people who have always known you in one identity that you are thinking of trying on another. Rick

Terry, who had always been a banker, "a numbers guy," was nervous about telling his friends, colleagues, and family that he wanted to own a vineyard. He thought they'd think he was crazy. But once he did tell them—and heard their support—he was even more motivated to pursue the change. Sue Burton Kirdahy's first public admission that she was interested in moving from financial services marketing to TV production was made haltingly to her husband's family because her brother-in-law, a Broadway producer—and possible networking contact—was visiting for the weekend. And she didn't even have the language for what she wanted to do. "I think I might want to be a TV producer," she told them hesitantly. "Wow," her in-laws responded, "that's really different from what you're doing now." When they asked her why, she barely knew what to say. But her courage in putting it out there was rewarded when her brother-in-law said he could arrange an introductory meeting with a friend who was a producer. As it turned out, the meeting didn't produce a job or even a direction, but it did give Sue a chance to talk about her interests, taught her something about the industry, and gave her the names of other people she could contact. Simply because it was first, it was an important stepping-stone on her path to change.

Part of what makes it scary to tell people who know you that you are thinking of trying something new is that it raises that old "exposure fear" we talked about before: *What if they don't approve? What if they laugh at me? What if they think I can't succeed?* But the fact is, until you talk about it, you *won't* succeed! You need the information and contacts that come from talking, and you need the support that talking can bring.

Just as important, you need to hear yourself describe your vision over and over again—because each time you hear yourself say it, something magical happens: you believe a little more that it will happen. The first time you say it, it sounds like fantasy—

me, a banker, becoming a vintner? By the twentieth time, though, with all you've learned, the vision will have evolved. Details will be added; the vision will be more concrete. With other people's stories under your belt, you may even be imagining the bridge from here to there. What once sounded like a fantasy is starting to sound more like the beginning of a plan.

But until you start believing in that plan, it will never come to pass. At root, we are all a set of self-fulfilling prophecies: we accomplish what we believe we will accomplish in our lives and nothing more. So practice believing in your dream career. Talk it up in glowing, confident terms, because the more clearly and often you describe it, the more you enable yourself to make it real.

Of course, some people will be naysayers. It's unavoidable. Some people just naturally leap to the negative, some will be jealous that you are making a switch that they themselves are afraid to make, some will always value "practicality" over passion. That's okay. Once you find out who your naysayers are, just don't talk to them about your plan. If they bring it up, gently change the subject. As Sandy Huddle said, "There are always people who will give you a hundred reasons why you shouldn't do something. I showed one friend my work and school schedule and she said, 'Oh, my God, how are you going to be able to do all this? It's too much!' I said, 'Stop right there. This isn't your schedule, it's my schedule. I chose this because it's what's going to get the goal for me. If you can't support it, I can't talk to you about it.' Another friend told me about kids her son went to school with who had left the TV business because of bad pay or benefits. I said, 'That's their stories. I'm going to write my own story.' If people can't be positive about my transition then I just can't talk to them about it."

Sometimes the naysayers are people who are close to you,

which can be especially hard. Sue Burton Kirdahy's parents were not supportive when she gave up her good salary and job security to pursue performing. What helped her cope with their displeasure was understanding that it was not about her so much as about themselves. They had each given up a preferred career early in their lives and had been unhappy as a result. She was determined not to repeat that pattern. When Joanne Bruner decided she wanted to buy a bed-and-breakfast, her husband was not at all supportive. He simply didn't understand why it was so impor-

ASSOCIATE WITH ASSOCIATIONS

When you do your online research, be sure to look up associations in your new field; they can be fountains of valuable information and contacts. Then, use those contacts! Most people join associations because they want to network with others who share their passion, so take advantage of their interest. When Cyndi and Mason Cobb decided they wanted to buy an inn, they researched inns online and quickly found the PAII, the Professional Association of Innkeepers International. Simply scouring the Web site, with its seminar descriptions, annual conference program, vendor lists, and bookstore, taught them a huge amount about the industry. It also introduced them to scores of innkeepers and consultants. Bit by bit, the Cobbs began contacting some of those professionals, asking advice, using them as sounding boards for their own ideas. Those early contacts later proved instrumental in helping guide the couple through the multiyear process of buying and learning to operate their inn.

tant to her. Her internal drive was so strong, however, that she decided to persevere despite his objections, and very slowly, as he saw her determination, his opposition lessened. Eventually, once she had done several inn-keeping vocations and was looking seriously at inns to buy, he offered to become her partner.

Fortunately, for every naysayer, you will find multiple supporters: friends, family, colleagues, and new people you meet through your research will rally around to prompt you on. Some will root for you because they love you, some because they wish they could do such a courageous thing themselves, some because they can't wait to become customers of your business! When Lisa Lathrop first began talking about the cheesecake business she imagined starting, she got so much support from people who already knew and loved her cheesecakes that she felt the business was sure to succeed. She was smart enough to know that her supporters were hardly a realistic test market, but their enthusiasm fueled her vision and helped her keep going. Some people will support you simply because *your* energy and vision inspire *them*. A friend of Sandy Huddle, watching Sandy do her research, decided she would investigate her own dream career and look into going to law school. Simply seeing the multiplier effect of her actions made Sandy more invigorated.

The support you get from the people you talk to will be so valuable that you won't be able to proceed without it. Every vocationer I've talked to has said the exact same thing: "I couldn't have done this without the support of——" and then they've filled in the blank with the names of family and friends who urged them on, who encouraged them when they felt down, who continued to believe in them and their vision all the way through the process.

WHEN IS ENOUGH ENOUGH?

How do you know when you've done enough research? There's no hard-and-fast rule. Some people love researching and won't be satisfied until they have file cabinets full of paper. Others just want to jump in and get their hands dirty with a vocation. Both are fine. You'll do more research after your vocation. For now, the time to stop is when you know enough that you just can't wait to move on to the next step, contacting potential mentors.

If you're not getting to that point—if you've reached "analysis paralysis" and, despite information overload, are still resisting shopping for a mentor—perhaps there's something else going on beyond a need for more data. It's likely that you're afraid. If that's the case, reread Chapter 2 and have a dialogue with yourself: see if you can plumb the deepest source of your fear. Addressing that fear head-on will probably free you to move forward.

Or it's possible that your resistance holds another message: maybe the career you're researching isn't your dream career after all. That can create its own form of paralysis. How can you walk away from that career after all the time and energy you've already invested? What will your friends, family, and associates think after everything you've told them? And if that isn't your dream career, *what is*? There's comfort in knowing what we want to do with our lives, in sensing what the next chapter holds, and releasing that comfort can be scarier than never having a dream to begin with. No wonder we feel paralyzed if research shows us that our "dream career" isn't.

If that is the case, try to relax and accept it. Another dream will come—just as this one did—but it can't come until you release the old one. In fact, having had this dream sets you up perfectly for finding the next one. You've already done the hard work of relinquishing the hold of the status quo. You've had the courage to publicize a dream and ask for help. You've become proficient at doing research. Who says the first dream has to be the "real" dream? Dream job seeking is a *process*. It isn't linear, it isn't left-brained. It's a circuitous path of back and forth, left and right, exploring options. The goal isn't to do or become a certain thing; it's to find out who you are and what kind of work meshes with your deepest self. As Sue Burton Kirdahy said, she began her research thinking she would be a TV producer because that was a title she knew. Two years and many explorations later she came to see that a job title is unimportant. "I no longer think about what I'm eventually going to call myself," she said. "Instead I think about the qualities I want in my life and I try to get those."

> "I am not afraid to change my mind. Everything I've done to this point has helped me in some way. I'm not afraid to say, 'I don't want to do that anymore.'"
>
> *Carolyn Walker,*
> *attorney-turned-jewelry-designer*

That should be your goal too. If you've gotten to the point where you've had a dream and learned through research that it isn't the proper fit, you have taken a giant leap in self-knowledge. You are primed to pursue your next idea. Relax and it will come.

4

FINDING A MENTOR

It was 2003, I'd been in Portland for almost a year, and my desk was covered with files on prospective mentors: dog trainers, winemakers, sports announcers, bakers, brewmasters . . . I was a walking atlas of dream careers in western Oregon—but I had never contacted one of them. I'd been too chicken. It was one thing to sit at home and scroll around online comparing microbreweries, looking for the "perfect one," and an entirely different thing to pick up the phone and ask one if it'd like to host a "vocationer" for a couple of days. Even the fact that I'd already done it back in Chicago didn't make it easier. That was a lark; this was for my own dream business!

One weekend I drove down the Oregon coast selling wine to restaurants. In the little town of Arch Cape, ninety minutes from Portland, I knew I would pass the Arch Cape House, a rambling, turreted bed-and-breakfast with panoramic views of the Pacific Ocean. My sister and brother-in-law had stayed there the year before and extolled its virtues, and I had made a mental note of it because inn keeping was on my list of frequently requested dream careers. I had promised myself that on my next trip to the coast I would stop in and introduce myself to the owner.

And now there I was, and I was nervous. As I drove south down Highway 101, gray ocean merging into grayer sky, the very idea of a bed-and-breakfast owner taking on a vacationer began to seem laughable. B&B owners already have their hands full caring for their guests; why would she possibly want to burden herself further by mentoring one of my customers? The honorarium I would pay wouldn't fully compensate her for her time; how could I even ask her for such a favor?

I got to the tiny beach hamlet of Arch Cape and found myself at her road, and realized I was narrating my own progress as if I were watching myself in a movie: *Oh God, I'm pulling into her driveway! Oh God, I'm getting out of the car! Oh God, I'm knocking on her door!* I barely had time to wipe my hand on my pants before I heard footsteps coming toward me and the door opened. A short, motherly woman who looked more apt to serve me cookies and milk than to laugh at my "chutzpah" gave me a warm smile. I took a deep breath. "Hi." I tried to talk slowly as if I did this all the time, "I'm Brian Kurth . . ." and I rattled off the little speech I'd prepared. When I finished, she didn't look at me as if I'd just proposed the most ridiculous thing in the world; she invited me to come in. "Oh, I don't have to come right now," I blurted. "I'm going to be in the area for a few days." Despite my practice sessions in the car, I felt totally unprepared for any kind of persuasive conversation. But she assured me that this was an excellent time, and before I knew it, I was sitting in the inn's big-hearthed parlor and Barbara was telling me how two years earlier at the age of fifty-nine, after decades as a scientist and teacher, she had researched inn keeping, vacationed with Arch Cape's former owners, and bought the B&B. Since then she had endured her share of troubles and triumphs, about which she was quite open, and I knew as I listened that she had a great deal to offer people who were considering a life change. I had a mentor.

Since that day my team and I have signed up hundreds of mentors. Some I visited "cold" just as I did Barbara; others I phoned or e-mailed first. Some heard about VocationVacations and contacted me. Regardless of how we found each other, they all have something in common: they intuitively understand the value of test-driving your dream. They all respond the way Barbara did when they hear the idea: *I'd love to help someone else get started.*

WIRED TO COOPERATE

Why are busy working people so eager to help strangers enter their business? Why are they willing to take time away from their work? To disclose trade secrets? To train their own possible competition? They do it for a number of reasons:

- They love what they do and they love sharing it with others. (Don't you get jazzed talking about the things you love— especially to people who also love them?)
- They want to give back for all the help they received when they were getting started.
- They want to give to others what they didn't get themselves, to spare others their own mistakes.
- They like the energy that a passionate newcomer brings.
- They enjoy the act of teaching and the pride that comes from being asked for advice.
- They believe in their occupation and want to see the industry grow.
- They're reminded that they have dream jobs themselves, and appreciate with fresh eyes how much they have learned and accomplished.

Beth Boston, who runs Every Day Wine, a casual wine bar and retail store in Portland, and mentors other would-be wine retailers, summed up the feelings of most mentors when she said, "In order for people to change their lives, somebody has to give them a chance. Somebody has to talk to them, inspire them, show them that it's possible. Someone really inspired me and I want to give that back. Yeah, there are certain fears or hesitations about mentoring, but then you say to yourself, 'What's the right thing to do?' and the right thing to do is to encourage people."

It's not really surprising that people like mentoring. Despite the perception that we are naturally self-protective—especially in matters of work, money, and survival—researchers have found that our brains are actually wired for cooperation. The act of helping someone triggers activity in the pleasure centers of the brain and literally makes us feel good. A 2002 study at Emory University in Atlanta showed how this works (*New York Times,* "Why We're So Nice: We're Wired to Cooperate," July 23, 2002). Thirty-six women were paired up to play a computerized version of a classic laboratory game called the Prisoner's Dilemma, in which participants play by either cooperating with or "betraying" their opponents. (The researchers used only women because few brain-imaging studies have looked exclusively at women, and to eliminate any sexual tension that might influence participants' behavior if both men and women were involved.) The pairs of women could not see each other or know what their opponents were choosing. Depending on their combined responses, the women could earn from $1 to $3 in each round of the game. If both players chose to cooperate, they each won $2; if both "betrayed" each other, they each won $1. If one cooperated and the other betrayed, the cooperator won $1 while the betrayer won $3. The financial incentive, therefore, was to betray rather than cooperate. To the researchers' surprise—and contrary to all rational expectation— most of the women chose to cooperate most of the time. Why? The researchers weren't sure, but scans of the women's brains might provide the answer: each time the women cooperated, the "reward circuits" in their brains—the areas responsible for feelings of pleasure—showed increased activity. The act of cooperating and feelings of pleasure seemed to go hand in hand. (Interestingly, when the women knew they were playing against a computer rather than another woman, they did not cooperate and their reward circuitry remained inactive.) Researchers believe, based on past studies, that neuroimaging studies of men would produce similar results. Did the women choose to cooperate because it felt good? Or did they feel good because they chose to cooperate? Researchers' opinions are divided. But on one thing they are in agreement: while we are helping someone, we feel good.

A study of infants offers another twist on the biology of helping. In 2006 researchers at the Max Planck Institute for Evolutionary Anthropology in Leipzig, Germany, were curious to see if very young children who had not yet learned social skills were willing to help strangers. While working with twenty-four eighteen-month-old toddlers, the researchers pretended to use books, spoons, clothespins, and other common objects. From time to time they would "accidentally" drop one of the items out of reach or mis-stack a pile of books in order to see what the children would do. Nearly all of the infants retrieved or replaced the misplaced item, usually within ten seconds of a researcher's "mistake," *if* they believed that the researcher needed the item to finish his task. If the researcher deliberately put down the items, the children left them alone. Next, the researchers made the test a little more difficult: they "accidentally" dropped items into

A MENTOR WITHIN THE FAMILY

By the time she was thirty-four, Beth Boston had sat in a lot of cubicles. She'd worked for an insurance company, a medical equipment company, and a winery; at companies with four hundred employees and companies with ten; but no matter where she worked, she was never really happy. She was always looking for the job that she wouldn't be eager to leave at five o'clock. In 2002, she was working for a dot-com start-up when the economy tanked and she was laid off. Okay, she thought, I can update my resume and go find another job I hate, or I can try to figure something else out. So she went off to live with her uncle J.C. Borders, in Moab, Utah. J.C. ran his own business—guiding tourists to scenic areas for photo shoots—but after ten years was thinking of getting out. Beth thought she maybe should take it over. Her plan was to work the business alongside him and see if it was a match.

For the next two months Beth and J.C. hiked the canyons and arch lands around Moab, guiding photographers to places of unearthly beauty. At night they'd sit in J.C.'s living room and talk. Although she loved the wild country and the rapport she developed with the clients, Beth didn't think a seasonal business in Moab was what she really wanted. What she did covet, though, was the obvious satisfaction her uncle derived from his work. "He was so happy," she said, "it was his dream. And that's what I wanted for myself."

J.C. encouraged Beth to consider working for herself. "If it doesn't work out, you can always go get that corporate job," he said. "I know you'll land on your feet." The fact that J.C. believed in her pushed Beth to take his advice. She returned home, determined to open her own business.

But what business? There were only two things she needed in a new career—to work for herself and to keep Porter, her black Lab mix, with her during the day—so the logical business, she decided, was to start a doggy day care. The fact that the local market was already saturated didn't stop her: she wrote a business plan, applied to the city agency that makes favorable loans to women and minorities, and was looking for a location when she met a man who was selling his wine bar. Curious about the business and the neighborhood, she went for a look and fell in love—not with the building but with the business! She knew she wanted to buy it. "I wasn't a wine expert or a connoisseur," she said, "I just knew that was what I wanted to do. After all my work experience, I was comfortable with the business side. I just figured I could learn the wine."

Nervously, certain he would think she was crazy, she went to her loan officer and explained her change of heart. To her surprise he said, "Just give us a good plan." Two months later, she submitted a revised business plan, got her loan, and bought Every Day Wine, a casual, bring-your-own-food-or-order-a-pizza wine bar, dedicated to the proposition that good wine doesn't have to be expensive. On day one, Porter greeted customers at the door.

That was in 2003 and Every Day Wine is still going strong—and Beth has finally found the job she loves. She definitely doesn't go home at five o'clock. "I work all the time," she says, "but I love it. I grew up with the attitude 'Monday through Friday you do the grind, Saturday and Sunday you live,' and that's what I used to do, but now I *live* seven days a week." Occasionally the old conservative attitude creeps in and she finds herself second-guessing her own entrepreneurial instincts. When that happens she calls Uncle J.C., knowing he'll give her confidence a boost.

In 2006 another wine shop moved in, just down the street from Every Day Wine. Beth lay awake at night, certain her business would founder. Finally she called Uncle J.C. "You know what that wine shop doesn't have?" he said. "It doesn't have *you*. Customers aren't going to disappear on you; *you're* the reason they're there." Uncle J.C. was right. The other wine shop opened, Beth's business remained strong, and in the light of that experience she was able to look at her operation more objectively. I'm doing a lot of things *right* here, she realized with an element of surprise. And since Uncle J.C. believed in her so strongly, she figured she might as well believe in herself, too.

containers with lids that closed after the item landed inside. This time the children opened the containers to retrieve the "lost" items as long as they believed that the researchers had dropped them by accident. "The results were astonishing because these children are so young. They still wear diapers and are barely able to use language, but they already show helping behavior," said Felix Warneken, a psychologist leading the study (BBC News, "Altruism 'In-built' in Humans," March 3, 2006). The findings led researchers to believe that helping behavior is hardwired into the brain. And, indeed, this makes sense. Our earliest ancestors needed cooperation to hunt big game, raise children, and gather far-flung plants. While competition was necessary to secure scarce resources for one's group, cooperation would have been equally essential to survival.

FINDING A MENTOR OF YOUR VERY OWN

So—mentors are out there, ready to cooperate with you. But how do you go about finding one? Well, fortunately, you've already done most of the work. All the research you've done to learn about your dream career has given you the names of organizations and businesses in your field, and every one of them may be home to a mentor. The trick now is to figure out which of those potential mentors is right for you. The process of selecting a mentor is really a mutual interview. The mentor checks you out to learn what you want and see if you're someone he wants to take on; at the same time you are checking the mentor out to make sure he's able to give you what you want. Here are some things to look for:

- *Passion.* First and foremost, look for people who are passionate about their work. As you call or visit people to interview them, look and listen for signs that they genuinely love the field. Who wants to learn from someone who's bored or burned out?
- *Expertise.* Look for someone who is an expert in the field. Perhaps you've already heard about someone with a sterling reputation. If not, once you narrow your search to one or two prospects, ask others in the field about them. How are they regarded?
- *Teaching ability.* Look for people who are good teachers. It's not enough to be an expert in the field; your mentor needs to know how to transmit knowledge to you.
- *Longevity.* If possible, pick someone who has been working in the dream job for five years or more. By that time the mentor will have worked out most of the bugs in the job or busi-

ness, will have demonstrated staying power, and will have a longer-term perspective to pass on.

- *Connection.* Most important, pick someone with whom you "click." You want to be able to ask *all* your questions, be entirely honest, share your fear *and* your excitement, feel comfortable, and have fun. In short, you want someone who makes you feel at home. If you have a choice between a more experienced mentor who's a little standoffish and a less experienced one who treats you like an old friend, go with the latter. You can always do a second vocation with the more experienced mentor later. Make your first one as comfortable and fun as possible.

MAKING CONTACT

Yikes. The easy part is done—the research and reading, the making lists of possible mentors—and now you have to do it. You have to reach out and make the contact. I told you my story about contacting Barbara Dau: I wasn't exactly Albert Brooks in *Broadcast News*—there was no sweat pouring off my face, and my clothes weren't plastered to my body—but I was feeling distinctly clammy. And I was supposed to be a professional! I know I'm not alone in getting nervous. Even the attorneys, salespeople, and senior executives I talk to get cold feet before contacting a prospective mentor. It's not just the thought of cold-calling someone to ask for a favor. It's that you're putting yourself out there, exposing your closely held dream. What if you get rejected?

Fortunately, the best way to start is not with a phone call, but by e-mail. Sending an e-mail will give your prospect a chance to digest the concept of mentorship without having to deliver an immediate response. It will also make your follow-up phone call much easier: the prospect will already know why you're calling.

Your Introductory E-mail

Short, to the point, and respectful are the qualities that will help your e-mail get a response.

- Keep it brief: the less your prospect has to read, the more he'll absorb.
- Be clear about what you're asking: I'd like to spend a small amount of time learning at your side *at a time that is convenient for you.*
- Make it personal: say why you've chosen him above all others.
- Let your personality and passion shine through: show your prospect why he wants to work with *you.*

Here's one way an introductory e-mail might go:

Subject line: (*your prospect's name*), will you be my mentor?

Dear *(name),*

For the last _____ years I have been a _____, but at the age of _____, I have decided that life is too short not to do what I really love. So I am thinking very seriously about moving into the field of _____. Before I do, however, I would like to spend a couple of days "test-driving" _____ as a career. I am writing to you because *(insert a phrase about why you admire this person and why you have chosen him as a possible mentor)* and I am hoping that you might be willing to mentor me, to let me come and work with you for a couple of days, at your convenience. I know that bringing a mentee into your business has its downside: even though I'm very eager to pitch in and do all I can, it won't be like bringing in an experienced worker. But I can promise you that I am a fast learner and that I will be VERY appreciative of everything you have to teach me.

I hope the idea of mentoring someone who shares your passion for _____ will spark your interest. If not, I will certainly understand.

I will call you in two or three days to discuss this further. Or, if it's more convenient for you, please don't hesitate to call me directly at _____. Thank you so much for your attention!

Sincerely,

(your name and phone number)

Preparing for Your Phone Call

Of course, you *will* follow up your e-mail in two or three days, just as you said you would, but before you do that, you have homework. You need to plan exactly what you will say. Planning ahead saves you the embarrassment of getting tongue-tied; it also prepares you to pursue the conversation in whatever direction it goes. The phone call may be very brief: the prospect may indicate clearly that he isn't interested and say good-bye, or he may be so interested that he schedules a longer call or meeting. Or it may last half an hour or more as you ply each other with questions. You want to be prepared for all three outcomes.

Here are some things to think through *before* you pick up the phone. You might want to write down your questions and answers ahead of time, just to help you feel more secure.

Your greeting. Once your prospect answers the phone, you'll have about thirty seconds to explain who you are and why you're calling. Fortunately, the hard work has already been done—by your e-mail. Now you just need a quick recap:

Hello, _____. This is _____. I e-mailed you the other day about the possibility of having you mentor me. Right now I'm a _____ but I'm thinking seriously about going into the field of _____ and I was hoping I might be able to spend a few days with you as your mentee.

FINDING A MENTOR, START TO FINISH

In the spring of 2006 I realized I needed a mentor in public relations. Prospective customers had been asking and I didn't have anything to offer. I also needed more mentors outside of Oregon. So when I realized I was going up to Seattle for several meetings, I decided to scout for a PR mentor while I was up there. But how to find one? I didn't know the first thing about the PR community in Seattle, nor did I have any contacts there to ask. So I went to my trustiest adviser, Google. "PR firms Seattle," I typed into the search window, and up came a directory of agencies with a brief description of each. Perfect! I culled names from the list. When I found firms that had been around for at least five years and had varied and substantial client lists, I checked out their Web sites. Ten of the sites impressed me with their quality and I e-mailed them, explaining who I was and why I was writing. I said I would be calling in two or three days but invited them to contact me sooner if they were interested. This was the same strategy I had used multiple times before to find mentors in everything from acting to wedding coordinating, and I was optimistic that one or two would at least turn into meetings.

Nonetheless, I was quite surprised the following morning to open my e-mail and find a response from Louie Richmond, CEO of Richmond Public Relations. Anyone who responds that fast must really get it, I thought, so I picked up the phone and called. We immediately hit it off. Louie told me that he had spent twenty years as a classical musician before transitioning to PR, and how much he would have loved to have a mentor when he was getting started. "If I'd had mentoring available to me, I wouldn't have made so many mistakes!" He laughed. "I'd be happy to help other people avoid them!" I knew he was the real deal. Louie went on to describe his firm and his clients and I could hear in his voice how much he loved his work. I had seen on his Web site that he was a marathon runner and suspected that he would understand the mind-set of a dream job seeker, someone who wouldn't give up at mile thirteen. Now the energy in his voice confirmed that.

The following week Louie and I met in Seattle and the connection we'd felt on the phone grew stronger. As he showed me around the firm, introduced me to his staff and showed me samples of their work, I had no doubt that any vocationer spending time with Louie would be in highly qualified and empathetic hands. The deal was clinched when he looked at me and said eagerly, "Sounds good, Brian. When will my first vocationer arrive?" He was ready!

Louie was not the only prospective Seattle PR mentor I talked to. One or two others called me back, and I called the ones who didn't. Some had no interest in mentoring; a few liked the idea but were too busy; a couple seemed more interested in the compensation than the teaching, and to those I quickly said, "No thank you." (Louie had never even asked about money, another sign that he was right.) So out of the ten I had contacted, one had been the charm. Not bad, I thought. Those were about the odds I'd come to expect.

Pause here and see if your prospect recalls the e-mail. He probably will: it's not every day one gets asked to be a mentor. Even if he has no interest in mentoring, he'll probably at least remember the invitation. You can also tell from his response whether he's interested in the idea, opposed to it, or lukewarm, in which case you'll have a chance to persuade him.

If, by some chance, he doesn't remember your e-mail, give the two-sentence synopsis you've practiced:

> *I've done a lot of research into _____ (or, I have a lot of experience in _____) but before I make a career switch I'd like to "test-drive" the job for a few days so that I have a better sense of what it's really like. I have a lot of respect for you and your work (borrow the sentence you used in your e-mail) and I was hoping I could come and spend a little bit of time with you as your mentee. I would do it completely at your convenience.*

Your follow-up. Once the prospect understands who you are, he is apt to want more information. Be prepared to talk about the following things:

- How you see the mentorship working: how many days, how much time per day, what you would expect from him. Describe your best case scenario (for example, three days, full-time), but also suggest other options (half days for one week, or two full days a week apart . . .) Assure him that you understand how busy he is and that you are completely prepared to accommodate his schedule
- Your level of experience in, or knowledge of, the field
- How you found him
- Why you think you want to move into that career
- Exactly what you hope to get out of the mentorship

Your questions. You will be interviewing the prospect as much as he is interviewing you and you need to know if you and he are a match. To that end, here are things you should be prepared to ask:

- Do you love what you do? (Just because the prospect is in *your* dream field doesn't mean it's *his* dream career, so check that out. I recently interviewed an ice cream store owner who had called me about being a mentor. That was my very first question, and, to my surprise, the woman answered, "Well, actually, it's been very frustrating and I have the business for sale." Within seconds I had deleted that appointment from my Outlook calendar and reclaimed the hour I had allotted to our conversation! Nice woman—but not a mentor!)

- What keeps you going? What is it that, every morning, gets you charged?
- Would you have time to spend with me if I came (or would you redirect me to someone else)?
- What kinds of things would you imagine us doing together?
- Will I be able to _____? (Fill in the blank with anything you particularly want to do or see.)
- Are there other people on your staff with whom I could or should spend time?
- Have you ever done anything like this mentorship before?

Chances are, you won't get through all these questions and answers in your first phone call, but going in prepared will increase the information you do get.

Calling Your Prospective Mentor

Okay, you've done all the prep, you're as ready as you'll ever be to pick up the phone. So how come your fingers are still shaking? Because not only are you about to ask someone for an enormous favor, but you may have an aggrandized vision of the person you're about to call. After all that research and all that preparation, you may see him as the Obi-Wan Kenobi of your dream career— perfect, intimidating, larger than life. But he isn't. He's probably

IF YOU DREAD MAKING THE PHONE CALL

Do you find yourself putting off calling prospective mentors—doing everything else on the to-do list first, deciding to check their Web sites *just one more time?* Well, here's a tip from the field of brain research: the longer you delay, the worse your dread becomes. In the words of Dr. Read Montague, professor of neuroscience at Baylor College of Medicine, the brain "assigns a cost to waiting for something bad," and the longer the wait, the higher that cost becomes (*New York Times,* "Study Points to a Solution for Dread: Distraction," May 5, 2006).

Dr. Montague was commenting on a study conducted by Dr. Gregory S. Berns, associate professor of psychiatry and behavioral sciences at Emory University (Emory Health News, May 8, 2006). In the study thirty-two people were put into a brain scanner while brief electric shocks were applied to the tops of their left feet. The subjects were then asked to choose how much voltage they would receive after various periods of delay. You might expect people to choose the longest possible delay simply to postpone receiving the shock, but they didn't. Seventy-eight percent chose a *shorter* delay in order to get the shock over with (www.webmd.com/content/Article/121/114414.htm, "Is Dread Driving Your Decisions?: Study: Dread Roosts in Brain, Often Prompts 'Get It Over With' Attitude,'" May 4, 2006). In the second part of the experiment, researchers gave subjects another choice: get a stronger shock sooner or a milder shock later. At first blush this seems like a no-brainer: I'll take less pain later, please! But more than a quarter of the subjects—28 percent—chose to get a *stronger shock sooner* rather than endure the dread of waiting. As Dr. Berns said, "The dread of having something hanging over your head is worse than the thing that you are dreading."

Studying the brain scans of the subjects, Dr. Berns noticed that in every subject an area of the brain involved in attention lit up before the shock was administered, suggesting that how much attention you pay to something "dreadful" affects the amount of dread you feel. Redirecting your attention, Dr. Berns surmises—distracting yourself with a movie, for example, before going for a root canal—may be one way to alleviate your dread. But a more effective way, if you have control over the timeline, would be to simply hasten the event. In other words, make the call to the prospective mentor sooner rather than later.

a lot more like you than you imagine. He's probably close to you in age and, perhaps, in family obligations. He's probably spent a similar number of years in his career. You're probably as expert in your career as he is in his; if the tables were turned, he would be calling you. There are areas in which you possess greater experience and wisdom than he does. So before you pick up the phone, give yourself a pep talk. Think of your prospect as a peer, not a paragon. It will make your interaction easier.

When you do call, four things are apt to happen:

1. The person won't be available and you'll have to leave a message.
2. You'll get a clear "Not interested."
3. Your prospect will lean toward "no" because the concept of mentoring raises concerns but he'll be willing to hear more.
4. You'll strike gold: your prospect will *get it*.

Let's take these situations one at a time.

If you have to leave a message. Say the same thing in your message that you had intended to say in your greeting. Just recap your e-mail, leave your name and phone number, and state a number of times when the prospect can reach you. If you don't hear back in two days, call again, and if need be, leave another similar message. If there's still no response after your second message, let it go. This is not the mentor for you.

If your prospect says no. First you have to decide what kind of "no" it is. Is it "No, I am completely, unequivocally uninterested!"? Or "No, probably not right now," which may really be a disguised "yes." If a prospect is completely uninterested, let it go. A reluctant mentor is not a mentor. You won't have fun with, or learn much from, someone who isn't enthusiastic about teaching. Put your energy into finding a better mentor elsewhere. But if the prospect says, "Not right now," it's possible that with more information you might persuade him. Take it to the next step.

If your prospect wavers. Here's where you need to take a deep breath and dig down into the part of you that is really energized and passionate about pursuing your dream—because if any part of you can convince the prospect to help you, it's that part.

First and foremost, you want to go for *connection.* If the prospect feels your passion, if he feels you are a kindred soul, if he sees in you his own early days in the field and remembers how much he could have used a mentor's assistance, he will be more apt to extend an invitation. Try to spark that connection by describing your own enthusiasm for the field. Outline your experience, describe your long-term vision, explain how the mentorship can help you move forward. If you connect on a personal level he will be more apt to say yes.

The prospect may also have very legitimate concerns about having you in his workplace. Mentoring you will take time out of his day. He may be concerned about having a novice underfoot. He may be reluctant to share proprietary information or train potential competition. These concerns can be understandable deal breakers. Sometimes, however, prospective mentors and vocationers can work around them—especially if a warm, person-to-person connection has been made. Here are some ways to handle possible objections:

OBJECTION: "I'm too busy."
RESPONSE: "I want only a short-term internship that works around your schedule—just a few days, or maybe just a few hours a week—whatever works for you."

OBJECTION: "I can't train my competition."
RESPONSE: "I'm not planning to open my business in your area. I'd be happy to sign a non-compete agreement saying I won't start a business within a certain number of miles."

OBJECTION: "It would cost me money to take the time to mentor you; I can't afford to give away my time."
RESPONSE: "I understand that you will lose productivity with me there. I would be willing to pay you a fee to compensate you for your time."

OBJECTION: "I can't have a nonemployee on the premises; I don't have adequate insurance."
RESPONSE: "I'd be happy to sign a liability release form if that would make you feel better and if would meet the needs of your insurance company."

OBJECTION: "My business is confidential. I couldn't take an outsider in."

RESPONSE: "I'd be happy to sign a nondisclosure agreement if that would help. Or perhaps you could let me see aspects of the business that are not confidential."

Of course, even with your assurances, the prospect is still apt to refuse. That's understandable: he's spent years working his business; he's justified in being protective. So if after a bit of discussion he hasn't started to agree, thank him for his time and let him go. You don't want a mentor who had to be talked into taking you; you want one who is excited about showing you the ropes. And you *will* find him—elsewhere.

If your prospect says yes. Eventually, you will come to a prospect who says yes. *Yes!* But hold on: your work isn't done. Now you need to figure out if this prospect is right for *you*. You want to get to know each other a little and see if you'll actually like being together. You'll want to ask the questions you prepared earlier about how the prospect sees the mentorship working, and make sure that your expectations are in sync. If the prospect is local, ask for a half-hour meeting. If he's long-distance, arrange for a fifteen- or twenty-minute phone call. When you get together (whether by phone or in person), listen *past* the words to see if you can discern the following:

- Does this person exude passion for the work?
- Is he enthusiastic about mentoring?
- Does he seem like a good teacher (patient, interested in you, willing to share information readily)?
- Do you *like* the prospect? Do you feel comfortable?
- Do you feel energized when you leave the meeting?

If all these things check out, congratulations! You've probably found your mentor.

How long should the whole process of finding a mentor take? Unfortunately, there's no rule of thumb. It could take two hours or two months, depending on how many e-mails you send, how many phone calls you have to make, and just how lucky you are. Many vocationers I know found their mentors on the first try: they had spoken to them earlier while doing their research and established a relationship, so when the time came to ask for a mentorship the path was already paved. Others found that even when they cold-called, the mentors were either so impressed by the vocationers' thorough process of preparing for career change, or so fascinated by the idea of test-driving a career, or so tickled to have been selected as a potential mentor, that they quickly agreed. Other vocationers found mentors quickly by pursuing a one-on-one relationship with a professional teacher, sometimes for a fee, sometimes for free. One thing I have found in my own calls to mentors is that the prospects who say yes tend to do so quickly because they really understand the value of the mentor role. They have launched or found their own dream careers and know how important a mentor can be. So don't spend a lot of time with a prospect who seems dubious or hesitant. Speed the process by moving on to the next person on your list. Your mentor is out there waiting to be discovered.

MULTIPLE MENTORS

Nowhere is it written that you have to have only one mentor. Once you've found your first mentor, and done your vocationing, you may decide there are things you'd like to learn or experience with someone else. A different mentor in the same field can give you another perspective on the dream job or a chance to practice what you've just learned. A mentor in a related field can give you experience that complements and extends what you've already done. You read in Chapter 1 about Sue Burton Kirdahy, who did multiple "experiments," as she called them, as she tried to define her dream career. Each experiment introduced her to an aspect of her chosen fields—television and entertainment—that she hadn't been aware of, and she investigated those aspects that interested her by vocationing in each one. "I felt like Goldilocks," she says. "*This* business wasn't creative enough, *this* one was too laid back . . . But I had to have those experiences to find out what was right for me."

Carolyn Walker, the lawyer-turned-jewelry-designer, also had more than one mentor. In addition to apprenticing with local jeweler Laurent Worme, who gives her invaluable hands-on experience, she established a connection with well-known jewelry designer Cathy Waterman, whom she met almost by chance. A friend, knowing that Carolyn loved Waterman's work, invited her to a fund-raising event at which Waterman would be a featured guest. Carolyn and her friend were milling around at the event when Cathy walked by. Carolyn's friend stopped the designer and introduced herself and Carolyn, and after the introductions, Cathy complimented Carolyn on her earrings. They were earrings Carolyn had made! For the next ten minutes Carolyn told Cathy what she was doing and eventually worked up the courage to say she would love to get Cathy's feedback. Cathy invited her to e-mail. Since then, the experienced and novice jewelry designers have conducted e-mail conversations. "I'm so amazed that this woman, who is so busy, takes time out to do this," says Carolyn, "but it's great to get her guidance on things." Unlike Laurent Worme, who offers hands-on mentorship, Cathy offers an "aspirational" experience that enables Carolyn to refine her vision of the jewelry designer she wants to be and helps her guide herself in that direction.

* * *

Karleen Savage also has multiple mentors who help her in different ways. Karleen had been running her own marketing firm for several years but was looking to make a change. She had a hunch that PR might be the way to go but lacked any real knowledge of the field. When she learned that she could vocation with Louie Richmond, CEO of Richmond Public Relations in Seattle, she thought seriously about doing so, but first she talked at length with a mentor closer to home. Pat Watson, a former Fortune 500 consultant, was the management professor in Karleen's program at the University of Phoenix, where she was getting a long-delayed marketing degree. Karleen had already discussed her marketing business with her, and now she turned to Pat for advice about switching to PR. They discussed the pros and cons, Pat asked many questions to help clarify Karleen's thinking, and then encouraged her to go to the mentorship with an open mind.

After two days with Louie, Karleen was certain that PR was the way to go. She imagined starting a firm that would be a "virtual SWAT team" for PR, a cast of contract professionals with varied skills whom Karleen would hire on a project basis to meet her clients' needs. She returned home eager to implement that vision. Ironically, she had done the vocation during the final days of a school semester (finishing her course work in her hotel room at night after her ten-hour days with Louie) and when she returned to school for the new semester, her first class was public relations. She took it as a sign.

The PR class gave her yet another mentor. When the instructor, Melissa Luke, praised Karleen's intuitive grasp of the subject, Karleen described her vision of a "SWAT team" business. Melissa liked the idea and offered to hire the company to promote a

YOU MEAN YOU PAY FOR THIS?

At VocationVacations I pay our mentors an honorarium for working with our clients. One of our earliest mentors was Myron Redford, winemaker at Amity Vineyards. Shortly after he came on board, I sent him two vocationers, both of whom had a great time, and a short time later I sent him a check for their VocationVacations. But a couple of days after I'd mailed the check Myron called. "What the hell's the check for?" he asked. "It's your honorarium for mentoring those two vocationers," I said. "You mean, you pay me to do that?" he exclaimed. "I thought I was just doing it for fun!"

project she was launching. She even offered her own team of consultants to work with Karleen on the contract. The company wasn't even launched and already Karleen had her first client! When the class was over, Karleen began working on Melissa's project, but the teacher-student relationship didn't end. Melissa continued to advise Karleen on how to network and build up her firm. She even referred clients and opened doors to potential business partners. The relationship had morphed, first from teacher-student to client-provider, and then into ongoing mentorship and support.

At the same time, Karleen found a fourth mentor in a man she had known for years. In the 1980s, while running a small company in California that arranged events for affluent clients, Karleen had made the acquaintance of Neil Cannon, the cofounder of Schmidt-Cannon International, a high-powered marketing firm.

Karleen had stayed in touch with him over the years and now she called him and asked him to review her plans. Neil, who had since started a new company, Aspen Marketing Group, responded in a flash, offering advice on marketing, negotiating, and taking risks. "Don't hesitate to call," he told her, "I'll help in whatever way I can." So Karleen began calling him frequently to check her thinking against his. "It's amazing," she said. "He has no business being nice to me, but for twelve years he has never pushed me aside. You'd think if you had dramatically grown a business in three years you wouldn't have time for little people, but he does. He is an obvious business mentor, and also a vivid character mentor for me. He reminds me of how I want to be."

So within months of conceptualizing her company, Karleen had acquired four very different mentors. Louie Richmond is her ongoing guru for the nitty-gritty of PR. Pat Watson is a business confidante, guiding her strategies and providing direction. Melissa Luke is her corporate development cheerleader who is helping her grow her firm. And Neil Cannon is her character mentor who helps her hew to the vision of the kind of businessperson she wants to be. She turns to all four on a regular basis; they are the hands she holds as she realizes her dream.

EVEN MORE THAN YOU BARGAINED FOR: FORMING A LONG-TERM RELATIONSHIP WITH YOUR MENTOR

Most people go into their mentor relationships hoping for advice, encouragement, and maybe a few contacts, and sometimes they come away with more: long-term business partnerships. Whether in formal working relationships or informal, ad hoc arrangements, vocationers and mentors often continue their relationships in ways that are mutually beneficial.

- *Mentor-turned–business partner.* Unsatisfied in her work as a prepress artist at a production printshop in Clackamas, Oregon, where, despite her own artistic talents and training, she sat at a computer all day setting type and preparing graphics, Paula Lewis fantasized about ways she could make money doing her own artwork. Faux wall painting struck her as a possibility, as did painting murals, but she couldn't imagine turning either of those into a viable business. Then she learned about Man One, a Los Angeles graffiti artist who made his living painting walls. She spent two days vocationing with him, practicing with a spray can and learning how he combined work for corporate clients with fine art to create a successful business. His single biggest gift, however, was his reassurance that at forty-eight, Paula was not too old to make it as a muralist. She left her vocation inspired. Back home she bought spray paint and Sheetrock and practiced, then cautiously began telling people what she planned to do. When the art teacher at her daughter's school heard about her business, the school commissioned her first project: a mural for the library. But Paula knew that if she was going to make it commercially, she couldn't depend solely on the community she knew. She would need to reach out to a wider—and younger—audience. But how?

  As a middle-aged woman living in suburban Oregon City, Paula didn't know the first thing about her prospective market. She did, however, know the work of a graffiti artist who did. On walls around town she had seen graffiti murals by an artist named Dizzy, and with a little legwork she was able to get his phone number. Did she dare call him?

Would he be flattered if she asked him for advice? Or would he think she was poaching on his territory and get angry? Nervously, Paula called him up, and to her relief he agreed to get together. As they toured the city view-

> "I'm always flattered when someone wants me to be their mentor. It's a mind shift to realize you actually have something to offer."
>
> *Beth Boston, owner,*
> *Every Day Wine*

ing his work, they found they got along; separated by twenty years in age, they nonetheless shared an artistic sensibility and passion. That first meeting led to others, and soon Dizzy had taken her into his world. He introduced her to other young artists; he expanded her artistic and cultural vision; he made her feel like she was an artist again, something she had long been missing. She began to feel more engaged, more challenged, more inspired. As it turned out, she had something to offer Dizzy too. While Dizzy was great at graffiti and had an eye for promising locations, he was less comfortable at reaching out to prospective clients. Paula, however, had no trouble asking building owners if they'd like a mural. So soon she and Dizzy began working together, garnering mural commissions that neither might have gotten on his or her own. Today, they both maintain their own businesses, but they frequently solicit each other's input and they bring each other in for selected projects. What began as a nervous search for a local mentor turned into a surprising two-way relationship—one that invigorates both artists.

- *Mentor-turned–business incubator.* Bill Winters (a pseudonym) has been an avid fly fisherman for thirty years; in the last three he's been turning that passion into a career. The switch began when he and his wife, Emily, realized that, at ages 47 and 45 respectively, they had enough money to retire from their jobs at a high-tech firm in just three years. Instantly, they knew what they wanted to do: move to Montana and pursue second careers in their fields of dreams: Emily in environmental policy, Bill as a fly-fishing guide.

With the three-year timeline set, Bill began serious preparations. First he talked to fly shops and guides and researched the business: he needed to know how viable a guiding career really was. Was there money to be made? What would it take to get started? Was the market in Montana favorable? Since he was also pursuing a midlife MBA, he wrote his thesis on starting a fly-fishing business. When he was through with his research, he knew he wanted to forge ahead.

But it was one thing to fish for himself and an altogether different thing to take others out on a river. He'd have to learn the Montana rivers, learn riverboat navigation, learn to manage people and equipment in dangerous situations. He needed a guiding teacher. At the shop where he'd bought his drift boat, people recommended an instructor who had been training guides for twenty-eight years. Bill signed up for lessons.

Over the next two-and-a-half years, Bill and his instructor Dave spent countless days together as Bill learned to navigate the boat around rock piles, to control it through rapids, and to handle simulated emergencies. Things that had once seemed daunting slowly became almost routine. Finally, he knew he was ready for clients.

Knowing it would take Bill a while to get up to speed in his own business, Dave invited him to co-guide with him in his own fishing guide service and he arranged for Bill to purchase insurance through him at a discount. Even though the formal lessons were over, Dave was prepared to keep the mentorship going by incubating and nurturing the start-up of Bill's business.

> "I love that people want to spend their time with us for two days. It's exciting to have them be so interested in what we do."
>
> *Tim Healea, mentor,*
> *Pearl Bakery*

• *Mentor-as-vendor.* Andrew and Laurie Mason knew they wanted to leave behind their long commute and rushed lifestyle in suburban Seattle in order to move to Oregon to start a winery, so Laurie encouraged Andrew to vocation with Linda Lindsay at Stone Wolf Vineyards. When the vocation was over, they faced some tough decisions: could they afford to buy an existing vineyard? Should they live on the same property as the winery? What would be the best situation for their two young children? Linda continued to offer advice. "Do you want to be farmers or winemakers?" she asked. "Winemakers," they answered. "Then you don't need to be growing grapes," she said. "Buy grapes and make wine at our place." So that's what the Masons did. They bought a house on four-and-a-half acres and, soon after, bought four tons of pinot noir grapes from two different vineyards. At the same time, they negotiated a rental agreement for use of the space and equipment at Stone Wolf. Within a few months they had incorporated and licensed their own winery, Sol et Soleil Cellars, LLC, and within a year of moving, they had their first vintage.

"Linda made it possible for us to become winemakers quickly," says Andrew. By first clarifying their thinking and then acting as their vendor, she enabled them to realize their dream years earlier than they had imagined at a fraction of the cost.

5

DOING THE TEST-DRIVE

Haneefa Malik had always wanted to own her own fashion business. After high school, practicality sent her to the Washington, DC, police force, where she became an officer, but four years later she moved to California and enrolled in an eighteen-month visual-merchandising program. At the program's end she went to work in her dream field, setting up merchandise displays in malls. Sadly, however, the money she made was not enough to live on and, disappointed, she went back to the DC police. Over the next several years Haneefa worked hard, investigating everything from prostitution to street crime. She liked policing, but she didn't love it; she still yearned for a fashion business of her own. But the job was a good job, it paid good money, and she couldn't bring herself to leave.

And then she had her daughter. "After I had my daughter I couldn't keep doing it," she said. "It took too much time from Ameera." So once again she resigned—this time determined to open her own upscale women's clothing store. "A lot of people said I was stupid to walk away. 'You have a daughter!' they said. 'You have responsibilities! You can't just up and leave because you don't like it anymore.' But it was *my* life, not theirs, and I knew I couldn't live with myself if I didn't try."

To save money for the store she sold her house and moved in with her mother. "My mom was my biggest support," she says. "I was scared. I thought, what if I'm making a big mistake? But my mom said, 'Do what you gotta do because you don't want to wish later that you'd done it. You might have succeeded and you'll never know.'"

So Haneefa set about learning how to follow her dream. She found a small school that taught basic business classes and enrolled in Entrepreneurship 101, where she learned the basics of starting and running a business. Once she'd gotten a business license and a tax ID number, though, she felt stuck. How did one start a boutique? She was starting to question the wisdom of her decision when she learned that through VocationVacations she could do a test-drive with Mercedes Gonzalez, a fashion consultant in New York. Two months later she was on the train to Manhattan.

Within minutes of arriving at Mercedes's office, however, Haneefa's dream took a nosedive.

"Why women's clothes?" Mercedes asked on hearing Haneefa's vision.

To Haneefa the question didn't make sense. What else would she sell? Women's clothing was what she loved.

"There are a lot of upscale women's boutiques out there," Mercedes pointed out. "How will yours be different? Did you consider children's clothes? You would have very little competition."

"But I don't love children's clothes!" Haneefa started to say, but before the words were out, she caught herself. In fact, since she'd started shopping for Ameera, she did love children's clothes: all the frilly little dresses, the pint-size blue jeans and trousers.

She thought about H Street NE, the DC neighborhood where she planned to put her store. It was true: there were numerous women's stores but not a single children's boutique.

"Why that neighborhood?" Mercedes went on.

"The neighborhood is up and coming," Haneefa explained.

But Mercedes shook her head. "There isn't enough foot traffic yet. You want to be in Georgetown or Alexandria where there's a lot of traffic and people are looking for upscale clothing."

Haneefa had been with Mercedes for less than an hour and already her dream had been jolted into reality.

Convinced now that children's clothes were the way to go, Haneefa went with Mercedes to a children's clothing trade show where vendors from around the world were displaying their lines. Hundreds of booths lined the aisles of the convention center—more clothes than Haneefa had ever seen—and as they walked up and down the rows, Mercedes explained the fundamentals of the retail clothing business. Shows like this, she said, would enable Haneefa to see clothes from most of the children's manufacturers so she could decide which lines she wanted to carry. The clothes they were seeing today were summer lines which stores were ordering now in March. Come summer, manufacturers would show their fall and winter lines which stores would purchase for the following season. Haneefa scribbled furiously in her journal as Mercedes talked. She felt like a sponge. There was so much to learn!

From the convention center they went to lunch, and from lunch to a second smaller trade show. There they talked to designers about the trends in children's clothing, they analyzed fabrics and manufacturing, and Mercedes told Haneefa what to look for when selecting inventory for her store. When Mercedes finally put her in a cab to her hotel, Haneefa was thoroughly exhausted. The prospect of actually opening a store seemed daunting, but at the same time, having it all laid out in front of her and hearing Mercedes's cogent explanations, she felt it was something she could master.

The next morning the tutorial continued, this time with a crash course in retail fashion numbers. Over coffee in her office, Mercedes explained pricing, start-up costs, break-even analysis, and other fundamentals that Haneefa would need to prepare her business plan. In the afternoon, she went with Mercedes's assistant to a manufacturer's showroom, where she learned the ordering process. As they sat at a table reviewing dresses, the assistant explained how to decide which styles to buy and how many of each, how to write up an order, and how to tailor purchases to her customer base. Once again, Haneefa took copious notes. As she had the day before, she felt that the information was coming so fast and furiously she would never remember what she'd learned, but on another level, she could feel the fuzzy, unformed dream she had arrived with crystallizing into a plan.

The day ended in Mercedes's office with a lengthy question and answer session. Haneefa was beat, but even through her exhaustion, she could feel her adrenaline pumping. Coming to New York she had held a fantasy; now she was holding a map. She had no illusions that following the map would be easy, or that she could avoid detours along the way, but she had an expert guide who had offered further support and she had a good internal sense of direction. She was confident that she would find her way.

AS THE BOY SCOUTS SAY, "BE PREPARED!"

Haneefa was so nervous and excited before her vocation that for several days she had trouble focusing on the tasks at hand. She's not atypical. Vocationers commonly find that for days ahead of time, they're barely present at their current jobs; their heads are too full of what's to come. But this is exactly the time when you need to slow yourself down and take a deep breath. Your vocation is going to be exhilarating, enlightening, challenging, and fun . . . but it also needs to be instructive. You want to come away with an accurate picture of your dream and a clear idea of whether it's the career for you. That means you need to go into the vocation prepared. You've already done a lot of research, and while searching for a mentor you thought through what you hope to accomplish. Now it's time to fine-tune that thinking a little more. You don't want to get home and realize that half your questions went unanswered.

What's Most Important?

Start by thinking seriously about what's important to you. You're pursuing a dream career because you want to live from your heart. What exactly does that entail? Does it mean working fewer hours? Or working closer to home? Does it mean making a difference in the world, or working with a particular population? Do you want to be indoors or outdoors? In the city or near the ocean? What are the elements that *have* to exist in your new career in order to make it your dream? Make a list of them—because after your vocation you'll compare what you learned on site to what you said you really want. In your vocation-induced euphoria, you may be inclined to overlook the fact that you said you wanted to work fewer hours yet your dream job requires round-the-clock attention. Your pre-vocation list can help you stay grounded. You might decide later to forgo some of those "essentials," but at least you'll do it eyes wide open.

What Will Help You Decide
to Pursue This Career Further?

When Karleen Savage considered switching her small firm from marketing to public relations she had two very specific goals: one, to get out of a field that required clients to change their way of doing business in order to successfully implement her advice, and, two, to get into a business that would generate a certain baseline income every month. When she went for her vocation, therefore, she knew exactly what she wanted to learn: how PR is packaged, priced, and presented. If she learned those three things, she felt, she would be able to make a well-informed decision.

Right at the outset she told her mentor her objectives and he tailored the program to her needs. "Louie was so open," she said. "I felt like I was sitting in his wallet! He showed me budgets and revenue projections. He took me to meet a client that had some controversy around it, and I saw how he curbed the controversy and resolved the problems. He showed me press kits and presentation materials and explained how his firm presents ideas to clients. He showed me things that ordinarily wouldn't be shared. I got everything I wanted and more." As a result, Karleen left the vocation with her two questions answered—and a clear direction for her firm.

So get out some paper and a pencil and think concretely about what you need to leave your vocation with. Your questions are apt to fall into the following categories:

- *Skills:* What skills do I need to learn or strengthen? Can I master them enough to truly succeed?
- *Money:* How much money does it cost to become qualified for my dream job or to set up my own business if that's part

of the dream? How much can I expect to earn initially and down the road?

- *Time:* How will I spend a typical day? How many hours will I have to work? Will that change with time? Will this job afford me the lifestyle that I want?
- *Technical issues:* What do I need to know about equipment, purchasing, location, suppliers, processes, etc.?
- *Pitfalls:* What are the biggest hazards in this work?
- *Career path:* How can I break into the field? What can I expect my path and timeline to be?
- *Family:* How would pursuing this job affect my spouse or partner? Our kids? Our extended family?
- *Support:* What organizations provide ongoing support to people in this field?
- *Contacts:* Whom else should I talk to?

GET PERSONAL: GETTING THE MOST FROM YOUR MENTOR

The answers to your questions are going to come partly from living your dream job—seeing what you do and noticing how it feels—but they will come equally from talking with your mentor. You'll get to learn from your mentor's personal experience—and that experience may vary considerably from the more public information you've already received. Conventional wisdom may hold, for example, that you need a master's degree to enter the field, but your mentor may tell you that she has only a bachelor's, as do others in the field. Though your research may have delineated a specific route up the career ladder, your mentor may tell you a backdoor path to the same destination. Industry Web sites may have suggested that the market in your industry is already saturated, but your mentor may know categorical or geographic niches that are not yet filled. Years of experience have brought your mentor several textbooks' worth of learning (including information she may not even know she knows). With a little forethought, you can access that data.

Your mentor may, in fact, have wisdom to offer beyond the job itself. Many people who do work they love (and probably most of those who choose to mentor) have actively chosen their careers. Many have made the switch from less satisfying jobs. They have stood in your shoes. They know the fears you're facing, they've dealt with the financial insecurities, they know what's involved in giving up the security of a "regular" job and moving into something new, and most will be happy to discuss this aspect of the dream job switch as well. So don't feel that you have to restrict your questions to the specifics of the job itself. Obviously, you need to respect your mentor's privacy—you want to ask respectfully and watch for cues that you might be prying—but give your mentor a chance to discuss her full experience. You're apt to learn important "off the record" information, and you may deepen your relationship as well.

For the same reason, you also want to tell your mentor about your fears and concerns. Are you secretly terrified that you don't have what it takes to make it in this field? Fess up. Speaking the fears out loud will disempower them. It will also give your mentor a chance to tell you how accurate—or inaccurate—they are. (Remember Sandy Huddle, whose mentor assured her she was not too old to start a career in video production?) Are you embarrassed to admit that, even more than the mentorship itself, you're nervous about traveling alone to another city? Say so. Your mentor will probably empathize and then give you detailed information that will make your trip easier. Are you nervous about simply being out of your comfort zone? No shame there: most people are nervous when they're doing something new. Telling your mentor how you feel will help you relate to each other as person to person instead of simply as professional to student. It will strengthen your relationship before you even arrive at your mentor's door.

BEFORE YOU GO: CONTACT WITH YOUR MENTOR

Help your mentor prepare for your vocation by providing him written information ahead of time. A list of your questions and concerns, as well as background information, will enable him to make the best use of your time. (If you've offered him this information in your earlier phone conversations, ask if you should follow up in writing. It might help him to have it when he sits down to plan your visit.)

Remember: think of your mentor as a peer, not as someone on a pedestal. You are as knowledgeable about *your* field as he is about his; in another context, the tables could be turned. More than one vocationer has found himself offering advice to his mentor from his own field of expertise.

Before your vocation send your mentor the following:

- your list of questions (See the box on page 117.)
- a list of anything you particularly want to do or see during your visit
- a list of your fears and concerns about the job and about making a transition
- your résumé or a short biographical statement
- a description of your experience and knowledge of the field
- a cover letter that goes something like this:

Dear *(name)*,

Thank you so much for letting me come and learn at your side!
Before I show up I thought I would send you a little bit of information. I've put together a list of questions I have about

getting into _____. I know our time is limited and that we probably won't be able to cover all of them, but it will give you an idea of the kinds of things I'm hoping to learn. I'm also enclosing a little of my background information so you have a sense of who I am and how much I already know about _____.

Again, thank you so much for hosting me. I can't tell you how much I appreciate it.

Sincerely,

(your name)

QUESTIONS FOR YOUR MENTOR

Here are some of the things you'll want to ask your mentor. Your own list will grow as you prepare for your visit.

Skills

- What skills do I need in order to succeed in this field?
- You've talked to me and watched me work; do you think I'll be able to perform this work well enough to succeed? (Hard as it is, ask your mentor to be honest; there's no point pumping time, energy, and heart into something for which you're not well suited.)

Time

- How many hours do you work each day? Has that changed since the beginning?
- How do you balance your work and nonwork life?

Finances

- What does it cost to get the required education?
- What does it cost to get set up in this dream job?

- Do you have advice about getting a loan or working with bankers?
- What are the biggest expenses? The most unpredictable expenses? The hardest to control expenses?
- Which expenses can I defray and which are essential at start-up?
- What can I expect to earn at first? Down the road?
- How long did it take you to break even? Earn a profit?
- What did you earn at first? What do you earn now?
- What were your biggest money mistakes?
- What has helped you maximize revenue and reduce expenses?
- Would you be willing to let me see your business plan? Your annual budget?

Technical Issues

- What do I need to know about equipment, purchasing, suppliers, location, building needs, technical processes?
- What ongoing training do you recommend?
- Are there any mistakes you made that I can learn from?

Marketing

- How do you attract customers? What works well? Less well?
- How do you determine prices?
- What were your biggest marketing mistakes?
- What was your biggest marketing success?

General

- What were your biggest surprises?
- What was your hardest time?

- What is hardest for you on an ongoing basis?
- What would you do differently if you were starting over?
- What is the biggest obstacle you think I'll face?
- What should I absolutely do?
- What should I absolutely not do?
- What else should I ask you?

Career Path

- How did you get into the field?
- What can you imagine for me?

Next Steps

- What are the next steps I need to take to move forward?
- Do you have contacts who can help me?
- Are there other people you recommend I speak to?
- Are there organizations in this field that I should join (or stay away from)?

CHOOSE A CHEERLEADER

One of the most intimidating aspects of pursuing a dream career is the sense that you're doing it all alone. Behind you is the security of the existing job and company, paycheck and lifestyle; in front of you is . . . *who knows?* You feel as if you're standing at the edge of a cliff and all the people with safety nets are behind you.

Well, that isn't really true. As you move forward through the process, numerous people will come forward to support you. You'll find bankers who can help you with financing, marketers who will help you with pricing, industry mentors who can help you learn the ins and outs of the business . . . As you pinpoint each new need you will find people to help you meet it, and those people will come to feel like trusted advisers. One day you'll look around and realize that you've created an entire support network to guide you forward. You will not be doing it alone.

But that's all in the future. For right now you need to choose one person—just one carefully selected person—to be your main cheerleader. This person will be your primary support through the entire process—the person you lean on when things get tough, the person whose judgment you know you can trust, the person whose vision of your future will remain unclouded even when yours starts to blur. Your cheerleader will set deadlines for you when you procrastinate; she will remind you why you're doing this when you start to waver; she will ask probing questions that help you see the forest as well as the trees.

In fact, one of the biggest reasons to have a cheerleader is that that person will be able to see things that you are too close to see yourself. Lynn Kindler, one of the VocationVacations-affiliated coaches, worked with a vocationer who was thinking of leaving a technology firm to start a vineyard. The woman had told Lynn that her three sons were within a few years of leaving home. As she described her interest in the vineyard it became clear to Lynn that what appealed to her most was the gardening. "It sounds like you're interested in nurturing things," she observed. Tears sprang to the woman's eyes. Until that moment she had not connected her sons' departures with her dream career. Now, suddenly, she saw her underlying feeling: she was going to miss her boys and was wanting something else to nurture! This awareness, and Lynn's gentle questions, prompted the woman to look even more closely at what she was feeling. She realized that although she had been very successful in her career, she had paid less attention to her own needs and desires, and that what she was being drawn to in a dream career was something that, unlike her existing job, appealed equally to her heart and mind. Operating a vineyard, with its dual aspects of business and gardening, fit the bill, and when she went on her vocation she was able to observe both her intellectual and emotional responses. After her vocation, a second career option came to mind. She was already growing small amounts of lavender in her garden. What if she started an herb farm? Not just a small backyard garden, but a commercial farm that would engage her business mind as well as her hands? Within a month of her vocation she had planted five hundred lavender plants outside her house. It was not a commitment to herb farming; it was a *step*—a step toward doing work that engages all parts of herself. Over the next few years she will explore herb farming and may do another vineyard vocation. It's even possible that a third career option will arise. But thanks to Lynn's simple observation she now has a much clearer sense of what she truly needs in a dream career.

Lynn's professional training may have made it easier for her to help the woman make that emotional connection, but you don't need a professional coach to play that role. Nor do you need someone with knowledge of your dream field. What you need is someone who is a good, intuitive listener, who can be objective, and who genuinely cares about *you*. You need someone who will set aside time to meet with you periodically throughout your transition, and who will see this as a "job" that goes beyond the parameters of your ordinary relationship. You should think of it as a job, too, and when you choose someone to fill it, you should evaluate candidates in your mind just as if you were hiring someone for a paid position. Don't consider just family and friends; go through your address book. Look for someone who has the right personality and skills. (See our suggestions below.) You can even pick someone in another city: face-to-face meetings are nice, but you can have your talks by phone. The bottom line: don't pick someone just because she's convenient; "hire" the best person for the job.

When you've identified your candidate, describe the "job" to her and ask if you can "hire" her to do it. You won't literally hire her or offer her money; you just want to let her know how seriously you take this, and that, by agreeing, she's making a commitment. Tell her why she was selected; ask if she'll be able to give you time (perhaps monthly half-hour conversations) over the next year. If it feels awkward or difficult to ask for this kind of attention, consider it from her point of view: she'll probably be honored that you asked.

Qualities to Look For in a Cheerleader

When you "hire" a cheerleader, pick someone who:

- you can talk to openly and easily about your feelings;
- has a positive, "can do" attitude and will encourage you to find ways past your hurdles, not become overwhelmed by them;
- believes in you;
- listens well and understands that this part of your relationship is strictly about *you*;
- is intuitive and can listen past your words to hear the deeper feelings and issues underneath;
- lives from both her head and heart; who can help you organize and pursue your action steps, but also understands the emotional importance of this change;
- will not be afraid to challenge you when you get discouraged or when you lose your vision and focus; and
- is not threatened by your determination to make a significant change.

SHOULD YOU HIRE A COACH?

Professional coaches specialize in helping people define and achieve their goals. If you're considering a major career change, that kind of support can be very helpful. However, coaching is a relatively new career and certification and licensure are not yet required in most states; as a result, people with varied backgrounds are free to hang out the coaching shingle. I have worked with excellent coaches at VocationVacations; however, I have also met coaches who would have been better in another line of work. So if you choose to work with a coach, be as diligent in researching, interviewing, and confirming credentials as you would be with a mentor.

Before you hire a coach, consider the following:

- Select a coach who focuses on career coaching rather than life coaching. A good career coach will consider lifestyle; a life coach, however, may not focus on your career.
- Talk to references. Ask them if they actually made the changes they hoped to make. You want to hire a coach who gets the job done, not one who is simply likable.
- Hire someone who has been in business full-time for at least five years. Since anyone can call himself a coach, you want someone who has verifiable experience.
- Interview several potential coaches so you have a basis of comparison. You want someone who is passionate about coaching, has concretely helped people in situations similar to yours, and with whom you feel an emotional rapport.
- Consider someone who is certified by the International Coaching Federation, but do not disqualify someone

who isn't. A coach with decades of pragmatic career-counseling experience may not have chosen to get certified. More important than certification is meeting the criteria above.

Be careful on that last point. Your first inclination may be to pick a very close friend, family member, or spouse. But sometimes the people closest to us have the hardest time when we try to change, and people who feel powerless to change themselves may resent our progress. Consider the impact of your change on the people you're considering and pick someone who is able to be objective.

You may, actually, want to pick two people. If it's hard to find all those qualities in a single individual, split them up. Find one person you can talk with comfortably about the emotional aspects of your change (your fears, your hesitations, your moments of discouragement) and another who can help you with the "business" side of the process.

Before you go on your vocation, talk openly with your cheerleader:

- Let her look over your list of questions. Brainstorm together to see if you can think of others.
- Tell her your concerns. *Her job is not to answer them* but rather to validate them simply by listening.
- Encourage her to ask you questions as you talk about your dreams. Her questions can help you clarify your thinking.

Talking to your cheerleader should energize you and build your confidence. It should feel safe, supportive, and constructively challenging. If it doesn't, go through your address book again, ask associates for recommendations, and hire a different cheerleader.

BEFORE YOU GO . . .

Before you head off to test that dream, make sure to have the following things *printed out* in your itinerary:

- the specific hours of your mentorship
- directions for getting there
- your mentor's contact information, especially his cell phone number (make sure he has yours in advance, too)
- a rough agenda for how you'll spend your time (subject to change as your mentor's business requires)
- what you should (and should not) wear
- what you should bring

GETTING THERE

Hopefully, this won't happen to you . . .

Joanne Bruner had just put down her tray table on her flight from San Francisco to Portland. She was headed to the Sandlake Country Inn for her vocation and was seven minutes into the flight when suddenly the plane shook violently and rolled from side to side. Five l-o-n-g minutes later, the plane stabilized and the pilot came on the PA. "Sorry about that, folks," he said. "We're going to be heading back to SFO. We've lost one of our engines."

An hour later Joanne was on another plane backing out of the airport gate. They had barely started to move when the plane came to a stop. Five, then ten, minutes went by. Finally, the pilot came on the horn. "Sorry about the delay, folks," he apologized. "We've got an indicator light on up here in the cockpit. We'll need just a little while to get it fixed."

Three hours later (four behind schedule), Joanne landed in Portland. Happy to be on the ground, she shuttled over to Avis to rent a car for her drive to Sandlake. As she was pulling out of the Avis parking lot, the arm on the security machine came down—smashing her car and simultaneously sending the pitchforklike barrier in the pavement up into both front tires. One hour later, after all the proper paperwork was filed, she was finally on her way—starting the almost two-hour drive across dark, unfamiliar mountain roads to the Pacific coast.

Finally, at 7:45 p.m. Joanne arrived at Sandlake Country Inn. Diane, her mentor, greeted her and listened empathetically to the story, then recommended a nearby restaurant for dinner. Hungry, tired, and eager for a good meal, Joanne drove to the restaurant. She had just placed her order when the lights went off, plunging the restaurant into darkness. There had been a power failure; they were no longer able to cook.

Remarkably, despite that beginning, Joanne (who believes in destiny) had a fabulous time at Sandlake, where she confirmed her desire to own a bed-and-breakfast.

Hopefully, you won't have a similar adventure on your way to your own vocation, but nonetheless, be flexible and plan ahead.

- If you're traveling to your vocation, arrive a day ahead so you can relax and review your questions the night before.
- Get a good night's sleep. Vocations are draining! Between the newness, your eagerness to learn, your excitement, and your nerves, it will sap a lot of energy.
- If you're driving to your vocation, get good directions and leave extra time for getting lost. Better to spend ten minutes in the parking lot taking deep, meditative breaths than to find yourself hyperventilating because you're running late. Take a cell phone with you so you can call for directions if necessary.

WHEN YOU'RE THERE: LISTENING WITH YOUR HEART

So far, you've given a lot of thought to the *information* you hope to get before you leave your vocation. But information is only half the story. The other half is how your dream job *feels*. After all, the whole point of doing a vocation is to get into work you love, so a huge part of the vocation is testing out the heart side of the package. Do you love being there? Do you feel that this is the work you are meant to do? Does some inner part of you sing while you're doing even the drudgiest parts of the job? (Remember Tim Healea saying he didn't mind going to the bakery at four in the morning?) That's what you need to monitor while you're there. And then you need to use your imagination. You need to imagine that you're doing those things every day—day in, day out—for years . . . How does the job feel now? Are you going to love cleaning those horse paddocks *every* morning (weekends included)? Will the chocolate shop still be your dream career when the mixer breaks and you have to stir your giant vats of fudge by hand? Will you still feel thankful that you bought the B&B when the maid quits and you find yourself vacuuming and making beds instead of chatting up guests in the parlor? Talk honestly with your mentor about the "yucky" sides of the job. Get a good handle on how much time she spends on tasks you would find distasteful. Ask how she deals with the parts of the job she doesn't love—or even like—and how she maintains her spirit regardless. Then think deeply and honestly about how you would fare in the same situation.

Ask your mentor to play devil's advocate. Have her describe several common "nightmare" situations and ask you what you would do in each. Encourage her to challenge your responses to make sure you see each situation in the most realistic light. Do you still think you want this job?

DREAM JOB JOURNAL

Once you're on your vocation, the information will come flying at you faster than you can imagine. You won't remember half of it unless you write it down. Get yourself a small notebook that you can carry easily and maybe even slip into a pocket, and keep it with you every moment. Don't be embarrassed to have your mentor watch you writing. She'll feel honored that you take her words so seriously, and she'll know how serious *you* are about learning her business. You'll have time for only cursory notes as the day unfolds, so in the evening go back and write a longer version while the material is still fresh. That way you'll also see the gaps in your knowledge that you want to fill in before you leave.

The journal is also a good place to write down your questions before you go. That way, you'll be less apt to leave the vocation with important questions unasked.

Also listen to your body. Sometimes our bodies know better than our heads what is right—or wrong—for us. Is the work physically comfortable? Can you handle it, day after day? And for years into the future? Talk with your mentor about how her body handles the demands.

MENTOR RELATIONS

Your mentor has invited you to come because she's eager to help you learn. Hopefully, she's planned a schedule that gives you great exposure to the business. But as welcoming as she may be,

YOU'RE ON MENTOR TIME

Remember, once you find a mentor, that you have to work on *her* schedule. Much as she may want to help you, her business will come first. Carolyn Walker was reminded of that when her mentor graciously declined a chance to get together.

Carolyn first approached Cathy Waterman, the jewelry designer, about sharing her experience and wisdom, in October 2006, and Cathy's response was "Sure, e-mail me," which Carolyn did. Cathy responded almost immediately. The two e-mailed several times more and then Carolyn mentioned that she would be visiting the area where Cathy lived and that she would love to meet for coffee. Cathy replied that with the holiday season arriving, and the award season right after that in early spring, she didn't have time to meet in person but that she was happy to continue the e-mail exchanges. Carolyn was disappointed. "Don't read anything into that," advised a friend. "The holidays must be her busiest season." When she stepped back for a moment, Carolyn could see that he was right and that her disappointment stemmed from her own insecurities, not from Cathy's words or actions. Cathy, in fact, had been nothing but responsive and encouraging.

if something urgent arises, her own business needs will take priority over chaperoning you. That means things may not always happen exactly the way you want. You may lose some time with her, or have limited access to parts of the business, or may find yourself wandering the building talking to other employees while your mentor tackles an unexpected problem. If this occurs, *your* job is to be gracious. Take advantage of the free time and use it to do one of the following:

- talk to other employees;
- closely observe various aspects of the business;
- catch up on your note taking;
- think of more questions to ask; and
- imagine this was really your job: how would you feel coming here, doing these tasks, having these responsibilities, day after day?

Respect for your mentor's time and schedule also extends to "after hours." Some mentors are happy to use the evening to extend the internship, answering questions over dinner or attending a work-related event. Others prefer to limit their mentoring to the workday. Be sensitive to the signals your mentor is sending out. If you sense that she's open to it (and you're not depleted!), ask if you can take her out to dinner so you can continue to talk. But also understand if she wants to call it a day.

"MAY I CALL YOU AGAIN?"

So you've hit it off with your mentor, you've learned more than you can possibly remember, you're practically giddy with enthusiasm . . . More than anything you want to continue the relationship. You want him to walk you step-by-step to your new career. Well, he can't. Much as he might like to, he has his own job to do. But that doesn't mean that he doesn't want to hear from you again. If you've established a rapport and he's sensed that you're really serious about moving into the business, he probably does want to keep in touch and encourage you along. The question is: at what level? That's something you need to ask.

Before you leave, tell your mentor how much you've learned and how much you appreciate his attention, and ask if he would mind if you contacted him again. If he says yes, establish some parameters. Calling every week and expecting him to guide your every decision is probably too much. (If he wanted to be a business consultant he would have gone into that line of work.) But calling once a month and talking for fifteen or twenty minutes might be just fine. Perhaps he's even open to repeating the mentorship after a period of time, or to doing something on an ongoing basis. Perhaps he'd consider a fee-for-service relationship in which you pay an hourly fee to work at his side. Or perhaps he'd take you on as an apprentice, accepting your service in exchange for the chance to learn. Think about what arrangement would work for you and propose it. The worst that can happen is he'll say no; the best is you'll get to continue working together.

When You Get Home

First, before you do anything else, send your mentor a heartfelt thank-you. (Sorry, I know this sounds like Mom, but you'd be surprised how many people just don't think to do this.) A note telling him how much the experience meant to you along with a bottle of wine, or a bouquet of flowers, or a gift certificate to a nice restaurant will mean a lot to the person who just gave up a portion of his workweek to help you.

Next, get out that dream job journal (which at this point should be full of barely legible notes that you scribbled furiously while following your mentor through his day, plus those neatly composed sentences that you followed up with later each evening) and review what you've written. This is your big chance to record everything you learned before it seeps away. So go over your notes, make sure they all make sense, and add any additional thoughts and learnings. Jot down the ideas for your own career that came to you while you were there. Write down any questions you still have. You'll create many folders of data as you go forward in this process, but your journal will probably remain a bible, a source of info that you return to again and again.

Next, memorize what you're feeling. Hopefully, you've come back from your vocation elated. Regardless of whether you pursue your dream career, simply spending time living the dream is enough to make people euphoric. It touches something deep, deep inside; some essential part of ourselves. That in itself is life changing. If you've returned from your vocation feeling this way, savor it. Let the feeling seep through every pore, because that feeling is the whole reason you did a vocation; that's the feeling you want to replicate as you create the next phase of your life. Don't make any rash decisions during this period; bliss is lovely but not necessarily conducive to clear thinking. Just enjoy your elation and wait until you touch back down before you start planning your next moves.

If your vocation wasn't what you hoped for, if you returned home disappointed, don't despair. You just gained a crucial piece of information! You learned not to pursue that career! Think of the time, unhappiness, and money you saved yourself by finding that out now.

Regardless of which way you feel—elated, disappointed, or simply confused—celebrate. You did it! You dared to dream, you put the dream out there, you took a risk and test-drove your dream career. No matter how you felt about the vocation, you deserve major kudos. You've done what the majority of people are too afraid to do. Congratulations!

EVALUATING THE VOCATION

A week or so after your vocation is the time to start doing serious evaluation. Your feet will be nearing the ground, your head will be clearer, you'll be back in the real world, where you can make more calculated decisions. This is the time for asking yourself hard questions—and giving yourself honest answers.

The purpose of evaluation is to determine if this is, indeed, your dream career. Perhaps you already know in your gut that it is or isn't. Do a formal evaluation anyway. Asking yourself the targeted questions below will help you look closely and honestly at everything you learned and will give you important information for going forward.

The hardest thing about evaluating your vocation may be being brutally honest. By the time you've done your research, found a mentor, talked it up with friends and family, and done your vocation, you've invested a lot of time, energy, and hope in this career. Consciously or unconsciously, you've created a vision of your future, and a big part of you is now counting on that vision coming true. That creates a lot of pressure to bend the career to what you want it to be—or to bend yourself to fit the career. This is a great time to get your cheerleader involved. Her job can be to help you resist that pressure.

As you think through the questions, ask your cheerleader to discuss them with you. Encourage her to push you beyond your initial answers, to probe the feelings underneath. She may hear things in your replies that you don't hear yourself and encourage you to be more honest than you might be on your own. If your cheerleader can't talk through the questions with you, write down the answers. Writing enforces a mental discipline that may make you consider your feelings more carefully.

A Word of Caution

As you do your evaluation, focus solely on how you *felt* about your vocation. *Do not*—I repeat—*do not* consider the impact on your

THE 4 C'S

VocationVacations-affiliated coach Will Wiebe helps a lot of people through career changes. He recommends that when considering a new career, you weigh the "4 Cs": cause, community, capacities, and considerations.

1. *Cause:* To be satisfying, a career must provide a sense of cause, or meaning.
2. *Community:* You must enjoy the community of people you work with.
3. *Capacities:* It must enable you to express all parts of yourself and to use your core capacities.
4. *Considerations:* It must meet your needs in other areas, such as pay, commute, and schedule.

Rather than evaluating these qualities strictly with your head, Will recommends that you consider them from four distinct points of view: your rational self, your emotional self, your deep self, and your body. We'll talk more about those four viewpoints in Chapter 6.

family or your finances, or the steps required to realize your dream career. Unless you're single and independently wealthy, pursuing a dream job is going to be fraught with family and financial implications, and there will be dozens of steps to take that seem all but impossible. Your "yeah, but" voice will be all over that like white on rice, crying "You can't do that! What about your family? What will you live on? But you don't know the first thing about running a business!" Those are excellent concerns. They need to be addressed.

But they don't need to be addressed *right now*. They don't need to get in the way of deciding if this is really the job for you. If this *is* the perfect job, you can work on finding a way past those hurdles; if it's not your dream job, there's no point wasting energy on them now. So do yourself a favor; don't sideline yourself before you even get started. Figure out how you felt about your vocation before you tackle the practical concerns, because often, when we really, truly want something, we find a way to make it happen.

Evaluating the Vocation: Ask Yourself . . .

- What did I love about this job?
- What surprised me the most during my vocation? Does that change my feelings about the job?
- What did I not like about this job?
- Do I find myself thinking, if only X were not part of the package . . . ? Is X so problematic that it reduces my desire or ability to do the job?
- Can I do this job day in, day out?
- What parts of the job are apt to get "old" after six months or a year? How will I feel about the job then?
- How does this job match up with my list of "essentials"? If I sacrificed essentials to pursue this job, would the sacrifice be permanent or temporary? Is the trade-off worth it?

IF IT'S NOT YOUR DREAM JOB AFTER ALL

It's possible that your evaluation will show you that your dream job was everything you'd hoped it would be. If so, go right to Chapter 6. Start formulating an action plan to turn it into a career. But what if you found that your dream job wasn't as dreamy as you'd expected? Perhaps there were too many aspects of the job that you found unappealing. Perhaps the rigors of the job preclude the balance you want in your life. Perhaps you found that you don't want to own your own business after all, or that you want to dabble in that area but not turn it into a career.

That's fine! That's all good news. It was precisely to get that kind of feedback that you went on your vocation. The point was to learn those things *now,* risk free, before you invested years and dollars in a career you didn't love. Your goal, remember, was not necessarily to make this job your career, but rather to make yourself happy, to find work that serves your heart. Your vocation has taken you a long way down that path. You learned how to research a career and find a mentor; you examined your values and lifestyle and determined what you want in a new career; you proved that you can stay true to yourself in evaluating future prospects. Most important, you've opened the door to change. *This* was not your dream career—but now you're a lot closer than you were before.

Acknowledging that your dream job wasn't your dream can be painful though. Not only is it disappointing, but it opens up a troubling question: *Now what? If this isn't my dream career, what is?* One of the pleasures of pinpointing and researching a dream career is that it gives you the beginning of a vision for your future. As long as you hold that vision you feel reassured: this is where I'm heading; this is what I want to do; this is who I am. When that vision crumbles, that reassurance disappears. You find yourself looking into a hole where you once saw solid ground.

If you find yourself facing that hole, you may be tempted to continue pursuing the career you've been focused on rather than admit that it isn't right. But that would be penny-wise and pound-foolish. You began this process in order to make yourself happier and more fulfilled. Don't detour from that long-term goal because of discomfort at this moment. You've already taken one of the hardest steps—overcoming the inertia of the status quo. You hatched a dream and made concrete progress toward it. Everything you've learned in investigating this career will help you find the one that *is* your dream.

Consider a Related Career

Before you completely write off this career, however, consider another option: perhaps there's a related career that suits you better, a career that has many of the elements you do want and lacks some of the ones you don't. Connie Madison vocationed with a horse trainer thinking that might be her dream, but she realized during her vocation that at fifty-seven she didn't have the energy or riding skill required to train young, undisciplined horses. She voiced those concerns to her mentor and he suggested she try horse breeding instead of training. That met her need to own and work with horses but decreased the physical demands of the job. Connie went on to purchase a small horse property and several mares, and now uses her mentor's stallions for breeding. Thanks to his suggestion, she feels that she has found the perfect career. So ask your mentor or others familiar with that field if they can recommend related jobs that may work better for your needs.

Reassessing Your Existing Job

Sometimes the best thing that comes out of a vocation is not a new career but a new perspective on the old one. More than one vocationer has left his test-drive with a surprising realization: the job I have is the one I really want! That's what happened to Mark Rogers. Mark tested a long-held dream by going to cooking school, and six weeks into the program realized that his passion could be simply that—a passion but not a career.

Mark had always loved to cook. Growing up in a family with a strong cooking tradition, he had learned at an early age to hold his own in the kitchen, and although he had made a satisfying career in sales, in the back of his mind he had always thought, maybe I should become a chef. When he was thirty-nine, he decided to act on that thought. Something was missing in his life—was it passion in his career?—so at the urging of friends, he enrolled in culinary school. Twice, however, he postponed entering, saying he needed to beef up his nest egg before he quit his job. But even he knew that wasn't the real reason; he was scared. How could he give up a career he enjoyed and where he made good money for one he wasn't sure he'd like and in which he'd probably never make as much? Finally, a year after he'd first enrolled, he quit his job and entered school.

A month into the semester he began to grow disillusioned. He had assumed that although starting wages were low, with his age and experience he would rise quickly up the ladder. But now, exposed to the world of commercial kitchens, he could see that this would not be the case. Instead, he would stand at a counter chopping vegetables for eight hours a day while he slowly worked his way up. And while chopping vegetables at home had a certain creative and Zen appeal, hours at the cutting board didn't offer the intellectual stimulation he needed in a job. When the time came to arrange his first internship, instead of pursuing a job at a local restaurant, he found himself asking his professor about catering companies that might need help with marketing. What am I doing? he thought. I'm supposed to be doing cooking but instead I'm trying to get back into sales!

Six weeks into the semester Mark was riding his bike through a city park when a light came on in his head: he needed to go back to his job. He had *liked* his job! He had loved the flexibility of visiting customers and making his own schedule, he had liked the money, he had liked having evenings and weekends free. None of those would be true if he were a chef. Right there on his bike, he pulled out his cell phone and called his former boss. "I want to come back," he said—and as he said that he was flooded with relief. Cooking was a passion, he realized, but it was not his career. His career was sales.

Mark was lucky: his old job was still open and he was able to walk right back in. But something inside of him had changed. "I got to do what most people don't," he said. "I got to step out and step back in, and that gave me perspective. What I realized was that there were things wrong with my life but they didn't have to do with work. My career was fine; I just didn't know it." Since then Mark has made other changes in his life, including ending an unsatisfying relationship. He is happier now and, with his new perspective, has renewed vigor for his job. He still loves to cook—on the side.

KNOW THYSELF

Mark's experience—his new perspective—is not unusual, or surprising. But here's something that may surprise you: the greatest value of doing a vocation is not the transition to a dream career; it's the insight you gain about yourself. Even people who never move to their dream careers find that the vocation process sparks a remarkable amount of growth and change. Simply going through the process requires you to assess your life, take stock of what's important, and create a vision for the life you want. It forces you to break out of your mold, meet new people, and learn new things. It gives you a chance to watch yourself in an unfamiliar setting, seeing how you respond and how others respond to you. It provides you a mentor and a cheerleader whose insight and honesty help you see things you might not otherwise see. The process of vocationing helps you reconnect with your deepest self, that place where dreams are kept, so that you can choose to live in a more whole way. So whether you decide to pursue the career you test-drove, or a different career, or to make no career change at all, consider your vocation a success. You will have given yourself an experience that has the potential to change your life.

Debra Piver had no intention of changing jobs when she did her vocation at Nantucket Natural Oils, a maker of natural perfumes and aromatherapy oils on Nantucket Island. Nor did she expect to change the way she lived her life. She just wanted to learn more about perfume, her passion and hobby. And for two days she did just that. Working with her mentor, John Harding, she investigated every aspect of the natural perfume business: blending scents, working the store, guiding customers on perfume decisions. She even created two scents of her own, one similar to the flowery scents she usually wore, the other a spicy "oriental." Delighted with the bolder scent, she named it Transformation. When the vocation ended and she still had two days left on the island, she chose to spend them at Nantucket Oils helping out behind the counter. Simply being there was giving her joy.

It was during a walk on the beach that the significance of "transformation" became clear. Debra had never really understood her interest in perfume—why she read about it and thought about it with such passion. But suddenly, there on the beach, far from the rigors of her daily life, she saw that perfume was all about *pleasure*. It was the antithesis of so many things in her life! At home, where she was education director for a theater, a job she

WHAT DO I TELL MY BOSS?

One of the benefits of vocationing is that you get to try out a new job without telling your boss. As far as she and your coworkers know, you're simply going on vacation. Even if they know exactly where you're going and find it a little odd ("you're using your vacation to visit a *bakery*?"), there's nothing odd about having a passion for baking (or wine, or dogs, or whatever your dream field is). Just tell them the truth: you want to immerse yourself in an area you love. They don't need to know that you're thinking of switching careers.

enjoyed, she was always *working*. "I go to work, I work on myself, I work out . . . I work!" she said. "But perfume doesn't improve me. It's just about pleasure."

Back home in Los Angeles, Debra wore her Transformation perfume and thought about what she had learned. She began to consider her life differently. Where was the pleasure in her life? And what was the balance between pleasure and no pleasure? Could she be doing more of the pleasure? She watched herself make choices and was startled to find that in almost any situation she was apt to take the harder rather than the more pleasurable choice. "I go to the spa," she said, "where I can get an aromatherapy massage or a lymphatic massage, and I go, 'Oh, let's not have the deep, relaxing, aromatherapy massage, let's have the lymphatic massage; it's the most medicinal thing on the menu!'" She decided she didn't want to live that way anymore and began to redirect herself when she saw herself choosing the "harder" option. At work she looked at which were the pleasurable and less pleasurable aspects of her job and talked to her managing director about making changes. When she produced a discussion program for school groups visiting the theater, and knew that it was age appropriate for children but not scholarly in a way that would impress her colleagues, she resisted her usual urge to work all night at making it more erudite, knowing that the difference would be immaterial to the children. In general, she felt a lightening, a relaxing of the rigorous, perfectionist standard she had always held, and a growing acceptance of the idea that her life could hold greater pleasure.

At the same time, she noticed something else. Every day she wore one of the two perfumes she had created. The floral scent evoked no comments, but every time she wore the Transformation, people responded. Women asked to buy it. A store owner asked to put it in her line. "Transformation was a much better perfume," Debra said with a sense of awe. "It was created with a sense of play and newness." That sense of play, replete with the relaxation and pleasure she was experiencing, had permeated the fragrance.

Debra had wondered, when she first made Transformation, if choosing a bolder perfume would mean that she could also make bolder choices in other areas. Now, back home in Los Angeles, she was finding that it did. The insights and freedoms she had experienced in Nantucket had followed her home.

MOVING FORWARD

And where are *you* now? Are you more motivated than ever to pursue that dream career? Or did you come away with reservations? Having done the vocation and evaluation, do you have a clear sense of what you want to do, or do you feel as if you've taken the long route back to square one and you're still wondering what your dream career might be? If that's the case, it's time to research other careers. Keep in mind that researching other careers doesn't mean you're going backward. Finding a dream career is an incremental process. It may take two or three vocations to figure out what job is right for you. Each one will show you more of what you want and don't want and take you closer to your goal. If the idea of doing multiple vocations is daunting, relax. The first one was hard because you were learning as you went along. Future research and mentor visits will be easier. If you've decided that you do want to pursue the job you test-drove, then turn the page. It's time to plan your path to get there.

6

YOUR ACTION PLAN

George Kelley and Paul Holje had talked for years about opening a bakery. They're both self-described "foodies" who love to cook and entertain, and they figured that their hometown, Grand Forks, North Dakota, needed a bakery because all the other bakeries had closed up after a major flood. But the bakery had been just that—talk—until George's job as a federal air traffic controller got outsourced to a private company and he faced an imminent layoff. Paul, an architect who yearned to have a firm of his own where he could specialize in environmentally sensitive design, was also facing slowdowns and uncertainty at work. When, at the last minute, George was offered a different job at the airport, the immediate financial pressure was relieved, but the experience prompted both men to "finally figure out what we wanted to be when we grew up." So in March 2005, at the ages of forty-two and thirty, George and Paul decided to get serious about starting a bakery.

They spent the month of March brainstorming: What would the bakery look like? What would it sell? What would it be called? They knew it would have a regional focus, taking full advantage of their location in eastern North Dakota, where some of the

world's best wheat, sugar beets, honey, eggs, and butter are produced. They knew the product line would not be the bear claws
and white breads offered in the supermarket bakeries, but rather
artisan breads and hand-crafted European pastries. With no
other independent bakeries in town, they knew they would have
no competition. What they didn't know was whether the kind of
bakery they were envisioning would appeal to the people of Grand
Forks. So in April they began to do research.

Their first stop was the Internet, where they ordered $1,000
worth of books: cookbooks, how-to-start-a-business books, how-
to-run-a-bakery books. They talked to equipment suppliers about
ovens and refrigerators and learned the pros and cons of various
kinds. They spent evenings and weekends baking, experimenting
with recipes and testing them on friends. Whenever they trav-
eled, they visited other bakeries and analyzed everything they
saw: floor layouts, case setups, seating plans, staffing, customer
service, and, of course, the products. Whenever possible they talked
to the owners and were amazed by the openness of almost everyone they talked to. In the sparse Midwest no one saw them as
competition and most were quick to share recipes and details of
their operations.

By the summer of 2005 the bakery had taken shape in their
minds. They felt ready to tackle a business plan. Neither had ever
done a business plan before and they found the prospect daunting, but in books and online they found sample business plans for
bakeries that they could use for templates. They also went to the
Center for Entrepreneurs at the University of North Dakota and
to SCORE, the national nonprofit organization that offers free
help to entrepreneurs. But even with all this help, they realized
they were in over their heads. There were too many unknowns.
Would people in Grand Forks like their nontraditional products?
How many would actually come in and buy? They realized they

were at a choice point. So far, their cash outlay had been fairly small—the money for the books and a little travel; the rest of the research had been free. But now they'd gone as far as they could with what they'd learned. Were they invested enough in the bakery to hire the expertise they lacked? They were. They hired a local marketing firm to help them analyze the bakery's market. The marketing team helped them define the target market (which they acknowledged was not everyone in town), and then, by looking at the sales base in the region, they made assumptions about how many would buy the bakery's products. George and Paul plugged the numbers into the business plan—and the plan suggested the business would actually work.

But something was still missing. George and Paul had done a lot of research but their knowledge was all theoretical. They were an air traffic controller and an architect; their assumptions were based on hearsay. They needed hands-on experience. So they went for a two-day VocationVacation at Pearl Bakery in Portland, Oregon.

There they got exactly the education they needed. In two, intense, hardworking days, they discussed recipes and bread production schedules, considered the pros and cons of different types and brands of equipment, and discussed efficient kitchen layouts. They analyzed case setup, seating, line control, and customer service. They got a primer in bakery accounting and marketing, and observed Pearl's determination to be a positive place for employees. They ran all their own ideas and assumptions past their mentors. By the end of the vocation, George and Paul felt they had taken the "fast track." The whirlwind two-day experience had confirmed many of their ideas, steered them away from others, and given them tips they never would have thought of. It was exactly what they had hoped it would be: the constructive confirmation of what they were doing.

Back home they moved into high gear. They had learned that

restaurant equipment prices increase 10 percent on January 1, which meant they would save thousands of dollars if they ordered their ovens, refrigerators, freezers, shelving, and other large equipment by December 31. Suddenly, what had been an unpressured investigation of their dream became a race against the clock. To order equipment they would need money to pay for it, which meant they needed a business loan, which meant they had to finish the business plan, which meant they needed to find a location so they would know what they would be paying to rent and build out the space. Fairly quickly they found the building they wanted; however, a major structural renovation was necessary to hold the twelve-hundred-pound oven. Paul, who had recently been laid off from his architecture firm, developed a renovation plan and budget and they plugged the final figures into the business plan.

With the plan finished it was time to look for a loan. They went first to the bank that held their home loan. With their good credit history and the positive projections in the plan, they assumed the loan would be a no-brainer. Instead, the banker listened to their pitch, thumbed through the plan, then said he didn't see why Grand Forks needed a bakery. Two weeks later, he officially turned them down.

Dejected, but undaunted, they went to another bank. There, the loan officer looked the plan over while they waited and then showed it to his boss. A week later they had a twenty-year loan. They then went to the Small Business Administration (SBA), which approved a ten-year loan.

They were now at the go-no-go point. The next step would be to place their orders for equipment—but once the equipment was ordered, there would be no turning back. Were they ready to take that step? Scary as it was, they agreed they were. If the bakery failed, Paul could return to his career (the plan was for Paul to draw a salary from the business while George, initially, kept his airport job), but if they didn't do it now, they would always wonder *what if*? So in December 2005 they ordered their equipment. They took out a new thirty-year mortgage on their house (which they had just paid off two weeks earlier) and wrote a personal check for $50,000. The bakery was about to become real.

Once the equipment was ordered, its delivery drove their actions. They had twelve weeks to get the building ready. Paul made a renovation schedule and hired the contractors. And then, just as the work was about to begin, structural issues surfaced that made the space unsuitable for a bakery. George and Paul were devastated. The lease was dissolved, but now they had $120,000 worth of equipment coming and no place to put it! Their realtor took them building hunting again but nothing met their needs: buildings were the right size but the wrong location, or the right location but the wrong size. The right building was simply not available. They were one week from calling off the equipment, eating their $20,000 deposit, and kissing the bakery good-bye when a building fell into their laps. It wasn't a rental property, it was for sale—something they had not considered, assuming they couldn't afford to buy. But Paul penciled a renovation plan, George ran the numbers, and, remarkably, they found that they could purchase and renovate the new space with mortgage payments that were just $36 a month more than the rental payments at the old one. They called the banker and he agreed to give them a mortgage.

> "The fact that we'd done a vocation was featured in our business plan. The bank liked that. It showed that we were serious, that we'd done our homework *and* our leg work."
>
> *George Kelley, co-owner,*
> *Dakota Harvest Bakers*

They now had five weeks before the equipment would be delivered. Five weeks! Paul's new construction schedule listed almost to the minute when each subcontractor would come in. George and Paul did much of the work themselves and Paul's parents came for the long Easter weekend to help build the case work and lay the wood floor. To the backdrop of hammering and sawing, George and Paul interviewed and hired staff and trained them.

On May 8, 2006, Dakota Harvest Bakers opened its doors. The marketing consultants had created a brand and logo for the store, developed a marketing campaign, and planned the grand opening, and from day one, the community responded. People streamed in, having heard about the unusual pastries, breads, and lunch menu. One woman actually refused to believe that everything was made from scratch on site. The business plan had shown the business losing money for the first year, breaking even in year two, and turning profitable in year three, but to George and Paul's astonishment, they turned a profit in the first month. At the end of the first quarter, even with unexpected expenses (a new hot water heater and additional refrigerators), they were still profitable. The business has continued to grow ever since.

FROM WHERE YOU ARE TO WHERE YOU WANT TO BE

George and Paul had a dreamy start-up to their dream business. They went from conception to profit in a year and a half—every entrepreneur's fantasy. Unfortunately, they are also the anomaly. Most people take way longer to get their dream jobs up and running. Whether they're starting their own businesses or moving toward jobs in a different field, most people make a gradual transition as they work their way past the numerous constraints that stand in the way. Family obligations must be accommodated, debts must be repaid, money must be earned and set aside, classes must be taken . . . Pursuing a dream job is less a leap than a series of incremental steps that move you closer and closer to your goal. What is critical to reaching the goal is making sure that the steps you're following are the right ones. That means having an action plan: a clearly defined and timelined road map that will get you from here to there.

YOUR ACTION PLAN: START WITH A LIST OF QUESTIONS

Neither George nor Paul had ever run a bakery—or any other kind of small business—so when they decided to open Dakota Harvest, they didn't really have the foggiest idea of how to do it. What they did have was a fire in their bellies for running a bakery and the common sense to know they needed to ask a lot of questions. Their questions became the basis of their action plan; as they set about answering each one, they moved closer and closer to their dream. And so it will be for you. Regardless of whether you plan on working for someone else or opening your own business, if you make a list of all the things you need to learn and know in order to make your dream job real, you will have mapped out a plan for moving forward.

Your questions will probably fall into several broad categories:

- *knowledge:* things you need to learn in order to move forward
- *money:* how you'll finance your new career, and how you'll support yourself and your family while you make the transition
- *timeline:* over what period of time you'll transition to the new career
- *family:* how to make your new career mesh with the needs and wishes of your family

Right now, all those questions may seem overwhelming—but that's because you're looking at them as a group. When you take them on one by one they become much more manageable.

In the charts on pages 152–160 we've listed some of the questions you may have, as well as resources to tap for answers. You will, no doubt, think of more questions of your own.

You don't need to tackle all the questions at once. Many people prefer to tackle the money-related questions first: without having a financial game plan, it's hard for them to take the rest of the planning seriously. Others find it hard to plan their financing when they haven't yet figured out what their educational needs are, what their timeline will be, and how their family will be integrated into the plan. You may find yourself working in all those areas at once since each area will inform the others.

For starters, go down the chart and pick the ones that speak to you—the ones that seem the easiest, or most pressing, or most interesting. Pick only a few at a time so you don't feel overwhelmed and work on them at your own rate. For each one you pick, set a timeline—and then ask your cheerleader to keep you on track. Your timeline doesn't have to be hard and fast, but without one you're much less apt to get the project done.

Remember: you're the boss here. You set the goals and timeline. This is your dream you're realizing; even at this stage it can be fun.

> "When people start to feel unsure, or unready to move forward, or when their resolve wavers in the face of big tasks or obstacles, I say, 'Think twenty years in the future. What do you want your legacy to be?'"
>
> *Lynn Kindler, VocationVacations-affiliated coach*

KNOWLEDGE: What do you need to learn to move forward with your dream?

You May Need to Acquire . . .	Questions to Ask Yourself	Resources	Examples	Sample Timeline
Job-related Skills or Information	What skills or information do I need? How will I learn them? Do I need certification or a degree or can I get by without it?	School Volunteer work Apprenticeship Part-time job in the new field	Mark Spoto opened a coffee shop (while keeping his IT job). He worked weekends part-time in another coffee shop to learn the ropes. Mike Fischbein is transitioning from IT to a voice-over career. He volunteers as an on-air host at a public access radio station while working his IT job.	Investigate schools (including tuition and financial aid) by March 1.

Business-related Skills or Information	If You're Planning on Opening Your Own Company		
	How do I start a business? How can I finance a business? How do I write a business plan? How do I hire, pay, and retain employees? What do I need to know about managing employees? What do I need to know about managing the books? Are there government requirements? Are there legal issues?	Books Internet (search "how to start a business") Organizations: Small Business Administration (SBA), community colleges, university extension schools, Small Business Development Center at local university, SCORE Expert professionals (accountant, lawyer)	SBA offers: • classes • workshops • online tutorials • publications • consulting SCORE offers: • free consulting • classes • seminars • networking • online support • kits	Check out resources on how to start a business by June 30.

(Continued)

KNOWLEDGE: What do you need to learn to move forward with your dream? (Continued)

You May Need to Acquire . . .	Questions to Ask Yourself	Resources	Examples	Sample Timeline
	If You're Planning on Working for Someone Else			
Business-related Skills or Information	How sound is the business? Are the owners reputable? What is the benefits and compensation package?	Google the company. Talk to people in the business community. Talk to people inside the company.		
Industry-related Information	Do I need to learn more about my new field? • competitors • size of market • geographic variations	Your mentor Others in the field (observe, ask questions) Internet Industry organizations	Jessica Caulfield gave up real estate to open a clothing boutique. She found most of what she needed online, and she	Prepare a list of questions and contact three businesses in this field by September 15.

	• trade organizations • latest technology • trends • legal and regulatory issues	Books (talk to your business librarian) Industry consultant	picked the brains of other boutique owners in her city to learn local buying patterns.	
Feedback on Your Ideas	How will people respond to my business? How can I make it more attractive? What will people pay for my products or services?	Prospective customers (talk to people everywhere you go) Others in field (observe, ask questions) Your mentor Marketing consultants	Mark Spoto asked people on the bus, friends, and people at work what they would like in a coffee shop. "It was fun. I'm a quiet person but I can talk about the coffee shop easily and forever."	Pull together a focus group to give me feedback by October 31.

MONEY: How will you finance your transition?

If You're Looking at Taking a Job in an Organization

Questions to Ask Yourself	Resources	Examples	Sample Timeline
What is my salary likely to be? At what rate will it rise? If I take a pay cut, how will I manage my finances? Will I have additional expenses (e.g., school, commuting, travel, supplies)?	Talk to your mentor and people in the field about pay scales in that industry. Make a three-year budget showing how you'll cover expenses at your likely new salary.	Connie Hilliard took a $10,000 pay cut to take a job closer to her dream. "Harder to cover expenses, but worth it, because instead of hating going to work, I now love my job."	Talk to three people about typical pay scales by June 1. Make a three-year budget by August 1.

If You're Looking at Starting a Business

Questions to Ask Yourself	Resources	Examples	Sample Timeline
What will my start-up costs be? What will my ongoing costs be?	Research start-up costs with your mentor, industry associations, others in field, or online.	Terry and Kathy Kurth started a lawn care company. They used a small inheritance	Through reading, online research, and talking with people, make a list of start-up costs by July 1.

How long before it becomes profitable? Where can I find financing? How much of my own money will I have to invest?	Take "how to start a business" course to learn about financing and make local contacts. Talk to several bankers about types and sources of loans and how to qualify; make banker a member of your team. Write a business plan with help from experts (mentor, online resources, SBA, banker). Talk to other small business owners about how they financed their businesses. Consider bringing in a partner or investor.	as collateral for a bank line of credit.	Find someone who can help me with a business plan by August 1. Talk to three bankers by September 1.

(Continued)

MONEY: *How will you finance your transition?* (Continued)

If You're Thinking of Going to School

Questions to Ask Yourself	Resources	Examples	Sample Timeline
How much will it cost? Can I go part-time in order to keep working? Can I get a student loan without first cashing out my savings? Will I have to pay off debt first? Can I reduce my expenses?	Compare several schools (look at course offerings, tuition, and financial aid packages). Research grants and loans that might be available outside the school. Make a budget and timeline for paying off debt.	Sandy Huddle financed school by: • paying off credit card debt first, • working part-time while in school, • moving in with her parents to save money. She also moved laterally in her company to be closer to school and negotiated new hours to accommodate classes.	Research schools by October 1.

TIMELINE: How and when will you transition to your new career?

If You're Waiting for a Certain Event

Questions to Ask Yourself	Resources	Examples	Sample Timeline
Do I really have to wait, or am I choosing to wait because I'm scared? Is there anything I can do to speed up the timeline? If I really have to wait, what can I do in the meantime to prepare? • get necessary education • do more vocations, volunteer, or work part-time in the new field	Industry associations and conferences (for research and networking) Business-planning resources	Lea Chadwell is transitioning from being a veterinary technician to owning a bakery. She volunteers in a bakery, enrolled in a two-year baking program at the local technical college, and attended Culinary Institute pastry boot camp. She plans to work in two different bakeries after school before opening	Make a plan for how you will spend the time between now and your "start" date. Work backward and create goals that will enable you to be ready to leap forward on that date.

(Continued)

TIMELINE: How and when will you transition to your new career? (Continued)

If You're Waiting for a Certain Event

Questions to Ask Yourself	Resources	Examples	Sample Timeline
• make contacts • research • make a business plan (using resources above) • make a transition plan in order to hit the ground running when the time comes • start your new career on the side		her own. In the mean-time, she is working full-time and saving money.	

DOES YOUR VISION MATCH THE MARKET?

If you're planning to start your own business, one element of your business plan will be a market analysis: are enough customers willing to pay enough money for your product or service to make your business profitable? That can be a hard thing to determine, especially if you're starting an out-of-the-ordinary business. It may be impossible to find sales figures to use as a reference. In that case, you need to be as open-minded as possible. Don't assume that everyone will love your product or service just because you do. Talk to people familiar with the industry and with people in your target market and try to gauge *objectively* if the market will support your business. It's a lot easier and cheaper to change your business model before you start than after you're suffering losses! If research suggests that the business isn't viable, get creative. How can you tweak the business and make it responsive to the market while still maintaining your passion?

That's what Dawn Casale had to ask herself when she realized that the last thing New York City needed was another caterer. Dawn had been the accessories manager at Barneys New York for several years when she realized that career advancement at Barneys would take her away from the things she liked best about her job: working with the merchandise, vendors, and sales staff. It was time to do what she'd been thinking about in the back of her mind for many years: starting a food-related business. But what? Her first passion was cooking but she didn't want to own a restaurant. Catering? That was something she could easily imagine doing. For the next week or so she imagined her catering company: she would do it from her own kitchen, keeping her costs down. She would do most of the cooking and delivery herself, hiring helpers only when demand required. She would market to her contacts from Barneys and, through those people's events, reach hundreds of others. With low overhead, a quality product, and a built-in marketing network, she figured the business was bound to be successful.

It didn't take long, however, for that bubble to pop. New York City was filled with fabulous caterers. What could she possibly bring to such a saturated market? For the next week she tried to figure out a niche that she could own. Cocktail parties and hors d'oeuvres? Already covered. Italian food? Too narrow. Vegan food? Yes, an untapped market! But one that wasn't interesting to her. By the end of the week she realized that even though *she* was interested in catering, the market would not be interested in *her*. She needed to think of something else.

Where was the market void? She decided it was in cookies. Not chocolate chip cookies or huge, gooey cookies, but small, beautiful, gourmet tea cookies. Cookies made from unusual combinations of ingredients, packaged in lovely, artful boxes. Cookies suitable for gift giving or party favors or for savoring as a special treat. As she looked across the five New York boroughs Dawn saw no business offering that kind of "cookie experience." The field was open. She decided to make it hers.

Her intuition was correct. Using the same model she had imagined for the catering business, Dawn opened One Girl Cookies in 2000. She did all the baking in her own kitchen and marketed by word of mouth to her Barneys contacts. She did the baking, packaging, and delivery herself. When demand grew, she expanded to friends' kitchens and hired a baker and a packager-delivery person. By her third year she needed to rent a commercial kitchen and in year five she opened a retail store. One Girl Cookies has since been featured in *Martha Stewart Weddings, Bride, Gourmet, Food & Wine, Woman's Day,* and other magazines because its unique products are so perfectly suited to their market. It is exactly as Dawn imagined: a quality product, beautifully delivered, thriving in an unfilled niche.

FAMILY

Being single has its advantages. One of them is that you're often able to make plans without considering other people's needs. But for many of us, that isn't the case. We have spouses and/or family members whose needs matter enormously, and we can't just decide to run away and join our own personal circus. A part of our strategy, therefore, has to be working with our loved ones to get the opportunities we feel we need. Every successful vocationer will tell you that switching to your dream career is far easier, and your chance of success is far greater, if you have your family's support.

Unfortunately, that support is rarely automatic. Even the most encouraging spouse is apt to have reservations—simply because pursuing a career switch can be so disruptive. Finances, children, the partner's job, the extended family may all feel the impact, and while you float around on your cloud of optimism, you leave your spouse or partner no choice but to remain planted firmly in the earth: *someone* has to think about the mortgage, the children, the in-laws, and day-to-day life. The challenge is to find a way that you can have your opportunity while your partner's needs are also supported. The key is open, honest communication.

Here are some tips:

- *Listen openly to your spouse's concerns, fears, and objections.* No knee-jerk reacting allowed! If something your partner says triggers you, take a time-out, go cool off, think about why you reacted so strongly, and *then* come back and finish the discussion. Getting angry or accusatory will not help your cause.

- *Take your partner's concerns seriously.* They are valid—even if you disagree. Discuss them with people who have knowledge in that area (not just friends who will agree with you). Be open to what the experts say.

- *Address the fear.* Recognize that your spouse's objections may stem from fear. Empathize with that fear. Find concrete ways to address it.

- *Compromise.* There are many ways to reach every goal—even yours! You can compromise and still get where you want to go. Do you need to keep your job longer than you want to? Start your new career in small ways on the side. Do you have to wait until your youngest child is out of school before you switch? Do all your research and planning now. Be creative as you consider your options and you'll find ways to keep your new career on track.

- *Establish clear parameters for compromise.* If you do compromise, make sure the extent and limits of the compromise are clear. For example, if you agree that you can start your dream career immediately but that you'll go back to your old career if it doesn't pan out, make sure the turnaround point is measurable. Name the date on which you will decide, or the financial threshold you will have to meet, or another tangible target you will have achieved, in order to continue with the dream.

- *Don't overpromise.* No matter how confident you are in your ability to succeed, don't downplay the risks or overstate the rewards. When the inevitable setbacks occur your partner will feel misled, angry, and distinctly less supportive.
- *Get help.* If you have trouble talking with your spouse about these issues—if tempers flare each time you have a conversation, or you revisit the same arguments over and over again without making progress—see a counselor. These are big, life-shaping issues you're facing. Both partners need to feel heard and honored, and both need to be happy with the outcome.

Negotiating your desire to move toward your dream career may not be easy—but it has a tremendous upside. It presents an opportunity for your relationship to grow—partly because it forces you to listen carefully and respectfully to each other, and partly because it gives you a chance to connect on the deepest level. You've done a lot of soul-searching in the process of researching your dream career and doing your test-drive. You've probably learned a lot about yourself in the process. Now is a chance for your spouse to do the same. With encouragement, spouses, too, can examine their dreams, needs, and desires, as well as the things that have kept them from realizing those dreams. Talking about those things together can help you grow in closeness, understanding, and respect. You may not reach absolute agreement on everything; after all, you are different people and want different things. But, ideally, you can reach a place in which you can say honestly to each other, "I disagree with you on this, but I respect you and I will support your decision."

If you cannot reach that point—if discussing your dreams broadens rather than shrinks the space between you—there may be underlying issues in your relationship that need to be addressed. Consult a counselor. Professionals can often help you work through issues that you can't tackle successfully on your own. It's important to

AGING WITH 20/20 VISION

Many people have long held that holding up a vision of what we want increases our chances of achieving it. Now rigorous research studies are showing that, at least in certain respects, that is true. The studies in question have to do with people's vision of aging, but they have bearing on how—or whether—we realize our dreams.

Becca Levy, a psychologist at Yale, is one of several researchers who are testing the effect of beliefs about aging on the health and vitality of elders. Their tests are showing that people who hold a positive vision of aging are apt to be healthier and less frail than those who subscribe to the negative stereotypes about older people being frail. In one study, after testing the memories of ninety healthy older people, Dr. Levy flashed positive words such as *wise, alert, sage,* and *learned* on a screen. Then she tested the subjects again. This time their memories were better than they had been the first time and their walking speed had increased. When she flashed negative words on the screen—*dementia, decline, senile, confused,* and others—and then tested the subjects again, their memories worsened and their walking speeds slowed.

Thomas Hess, a psychology professor at North Carolina State University, saw similar results in his own studies. He found that when older people were told something negative about aging (for example, that aging causes memory loss) they subsequently performed worse on memory tests than they had in their initial screening. If they were first told something positive about aging (for example, there is little decline in memory with age) they performed significantly better.

In a separate study to examine the *long-term* effects of positive and negative visions of aging, Becca Levy analyzed the results of the Ohio Longitudinal Study of Aging and Retirement, a two-decade study of 1,157 people age fifty and older. In addition to health information, the study had included beliefs about aging, and Dr. Levy found that people who had more positive views about aging were healthier than those with negative views, and lived 7.6 years longer. They also had less hearing loss three years into the study than they had had when the study first began. These results persisted even when Dr. Levy accounted for participants' health at the start of the study as well as their age, gender, and socioeconomic status. (All studies reported in the *New York Times*, "Old but Not Frail: A Matter of Heart and Head," October 5, 2006.)

If maintaining a positive vision of aging can have a measurable impact on our health and lifespan, can envisioning ourselves in our dream jobs have an impact on our careers? That research hasn't yet been done, but the implication for dream job seekers seems clear: create a vision of your new career and hold it dear because our beliefs do, indeed, shape our behavior.

address those issues *before* you proceed with your dream because, unresolved, they're apt to undermine you down the road.

Meeting the Family's Needs
While Also Meeting Your Own

Inevitably, when one person in a family makes a significant change, that change reverberates throughout the family. Working with your partner, anticipate the changes your career transition will bring and plan solutions.

The chart on pages 168–173 includes some of the issues you're likely to face. It's not exhaustive but it will give you ideas for getting started.

How will your career transition affect your family?

	Questions to Ask Yourself	Possible Solutions	Possible Actions	Story
Money	Will I be earning less money? Will I need to spend a lot of money? What will that mean for our family? Can we reduce our expenses? Can we supplement our income in some way? How much of our savings, home equity, and/or retirement can/ should we use?	To reduce financial impact: • Keep existing job longer and start new job or school on the side • Take a part-time job while starting new career or school • Work extra shifts or a second job for a period of time to save additional money before switching	Make a multi-year budget showing how you will meet all expenses during transition. Agree to tentative timeline for transitioning in stages, as finances permit.	In order to finance their transition to the bakery, George and Paul decided that one of them would need to keep his job. Now, two years in, George still works full-time for the FAA. After an early shift at the airport, he arrives at the bakery at 2:00 p.m. and works through closing at 7:30.

		• Agree to an earning swap with your partner in which he agrees to earn more money now in exchange for you doing so later. • Slow your transition time-line while you stockpile money. • Pay off credit cards.		
Logistics	Will my new career (or transition) take time away from my family? How will I cover my family responsibilities?	Block out a day each weekend for family activities. Always be available at children's bedtime.	Make an agreement that covers each area in which you and your partner have concerns.	Mark Spoto and his wife, Angela, wanted to make sure that Mark's new coffee shop would not take him away from

(Continued)

How will your career transition affect your family? (Continued)

	Questions to Ask Yourself	Possible Solutions	Possible Actions	Story
Logistics	How will I provide quality time for the family?	Have a weekly date with your spouse. Involve family members in aspects of your new career. If working from home, spend a little time with your children when they come home from school. Have one meal a day with the family (with the TV off).	Make an agreement that covers each area in which you and your partner have concerns.	the family, so from the outset, they made it a family endeavor. Angela (who worked and was in school) did the franchise training with Mark and then did the hiring. Their daughter, Annette, and son, Anthony, were asked for input throughout the start-up process and earn money by working in the shop.

Risk Tolerance	If your partner is less risk-tolerant than you, can you find ways to minimize the risk?	Start smaller than you'd imagined. Talk to a banker and a financial planner about other ways to minimize financial risk.	Agree on a turn-around point that your partner can live with: an amount of money and time you will not go beyond.	Mark Spoto had originally intended to open an independent coffee shop, but when his wife grew nervous about the risk, he bought a Dunn Brothers franchise instead.
Your Relationship	Do I understand my spouse's concerns? Can I appreciate and respect my spouse's concerns? Can we talk about this calmly, without fear or anger?	If your honest answer to most of these questions is "no," consider letting a marriage counselor help you strengthen your communication.	Talk to friends, clergy, a school nurse, your doctor, or your health insurer to find a licensed mental health professional. You may want to look specifically for	When Mary Dunn decided at fifty-two to pursue acting alongside her banking job, it sent shock waves through her marriage. The decision had come from the

(Continued)

How will your career transition affect your family? (Continued)

Your Relationship	Questions to Ask Yourself	Possible Solutions	Possible Actions	Story
	Are we usually able to support each other even when we disagree? Do we tend to compromise equally in our relationship? Are we both willing to make compromises in this situation? Do we both feel heard, seen, understood, and respected?	If your honest answer to most of these questions is "no," consider letting a marriage counselor help you strengthen your communication.	a licensed marriage and family therapist (LMFT).	part of Mary that had been hidden for twenty-five years, a part that felt unrecognized in the marriage. As a result, Mary and her husband began to examine deep-seated issues that they had long brushed aside. They are trying to under-stand and

support each other more fully, but changing old patterns does not come easily.

Does my partner understand how important this is to me, and why?
Do we both have room to grow and change in this relationship?
Do we both feel equal in the relationship?

Making Decisions *for* All of You and *with* All of You

The process of pursuing a dream job involves a host of difficult decisions: Should I cut back my hours? Should I spend the money to go to school? Should we move the children? Should we buy this property? Often in life we make decisions from our necks up, as if all that mattered was our thoughts. But career decisions are not purely rational; they affect how we and other people feel. And (as you well know if you've been negotiating with a spouse or partner) those feelings must be taken into account. Some people are able to monitor their emotions effortlessly; they *feel* a decision first and analyze it later. But for others the process is not so simple.

For many of us it's surprisingly easy to hide our feelings from ourselves. We convince ourselves that what we've decided with our heads is also what we want in our hearts when, in fact, our hearts may want something entirely different. We may do that to please our family (it's easier "not to know" what we feel than to acknowledge feelings that might rock the boat); or because we grew up in a family where we learned, directly or indirectly, not to express our strongest feelings; or because we're afraid of what we might find if we look inside (those "dark" feelings of unhappiness, fear, sadness, anger, and grief can seem particularly scary). But the hazard in not addressing our feelings when we make big decisions is that later, once we're living with the decision, those feelings often come out to haunt us. You probably know people who chose a job, or a career, or even a spouse, because their heads propelled them into that decision, only to discover later that in their hearts they were unhappy.

VocationVacations-affiliated coach Will Wiebe works with a method for helping people avoid that problem and look holistically at their decisions. He suggests that people consider four aspects of themselves when making career decisions: the rational

INCLUDING THE CHILDREN

When Karleen Savage decided to switch her marketing firm to PR, she was also making a decision to expand the size and scope of her business. She knew it would take more of her time and energy, which would in turn mean sacrifices for her seven children. So before she made her final decision she sat the kids down and explained the situation. "Here's what I want to do," she said, "but I need your support. You might have to deal with less for right now. You might have to take care of yourselves and be more responsible instead of relying on my input all the time. It will take a lot of independence and discipline." Then they went around the room and each of the children, whose ages varied from ten to sixteen, asked questions and voiced concerns. "Will we still be able to take vacations?" they asked. "Will we have to move?" "Will you still be able to come see my games?" Karleen addressed each of their concerns as honestly as she could and they voted. All seven voted yes. "Okay," Karleen said. "There's no turning back."

self, the emotional self, the body, and the deep self. When all four parts are considered, your decisions are much more likely to feel right over the long term.

To help determine how all four parts of you feel, ask yourself the following questions:

- *Your rational self:* Does this decision make sense logically, financially, logistically? Will it position me well for the future? Do the risks outweigh the gains? Do I understand the consequences? Have I been able to get satisfying answers to my questions and reservations?

- *Your emotional self:* How do I feel as a result of this decision: Peaceful? Liberated? Fearful? Anxious? If I feel a mix of feelings, which predominate?
- *Your body:* What physical sensations are awakened by this decision: A sense of energy? Relaxation? Tension? Shallow breathing? A lump in the throat? An inability to sleep? A tightening of the chest?
- *Your deep self:* Does this decision honor who I am in my core? Does it make me feel whole?

You'll know you've made the right decision if:

- it feels right in your core;
- it meshes with your deep aspirations;
- you feel good about it (there may be elements you're not crazy about but you know you can live with them); and
- you feel committed to it and can visualize yourself carrying it out.

FIND SUPPORTERS

If it's hard to make a career transition without the full support of your family, it's *impossible* to do it without the guidance of outside fans, allies, and experts. Earlier in this process you "hired" a cheerleader to help keep you going and clarify your thinking; now it's time to get that person backups. You need people who will urge you on, ask tough questions, and supply perspective and information that you can't get on your own. You need both *personal* and *professional* supporters.

Personal supporters are friends, family, and colleagues, the people who love you and care about you and want to see you succeed. Their job is to egg you on, remind you why you're doing this, and tell you how badly the world needs you to make this change. (Remember Toni Cory in Chapter 1, who said that what kept her going in rough times was all the people who couldn't wait to bring their dogs to her day care?) Talk up your new career to anyone you think will be supportive; get as many supporters as you can find.

Professional supporters are experts in the areas where you need help. They may be paid professionals (lawyers, accountants, financial planners, industry consultants, business plan consultants, marketing consultants . . . depending on your needs). Or they may be volunteers (your SBA teacher if you took a course, a SCORE volunteer, your local chamber of commerce, contacts you've made in the field, friends with skills you need . . .). Your banker should be one of your biggest supporters; he's watched many businesses come and go and has a professional interest in seeing yours succeed, so take advantage of his interest and knowledge.

It may be hard to ask for help. People who have the courage to pursue their dream jobs are often the same people who feel they should do everything themselves. If that's you, try to resist that urge. You're not in Kansas anymore! You're moving into a whole new field and there's lots you don't yet know. Eventually you'll be as expert in the new field as you are in your old one, but right now, the more you let yourself learn from others, the faster that day will come.

That said, however, choose your supporters wisely. Your new venture is fragile, and a little skepticism from a critical few can go a long way toward deflating your determination. So think twice before sharing your plans. People who are risk averse or generally negative about change will not make good supporters. People who are invested in seeing you "the old way" or who feel threatened by your change are also not good candidates. Professionals who give you advice that seems questionable may not be good supporters either. Just because they're professionals doesn't mean they're right. Get a second opinion.

BE CAREFUL WHOM YOU TALK TO: OTHER PEOPLE'S OPINIONS CAN CHANGE YOUR MIND!

According to research, other people's opinions can literally change the way you see. In a research study done by Dr. Gregory Berns at Emory University in Atlanta in 2005, thirty-two laboratory volunteers were asked to mentally rotate computer images of three-dimensional objects to determine if the objects were the same or different. Before stating their decisions, they heard the decisions of four other volunteers who they believed were also research subjects but who were actually actors working with the researchers. Sometimes those actors deliberately gave unanimous wrong answers, and 41 percent of the time the research subjects went along with the group's decision, even when it was fairly obvious that the answer was wrong.

When the researchers studied the subjects' brains with a functional MRI scanner, they found that each time a subject acted independently of the group, the scanner showed brain activity in the areas devoted to emotion. Apparently, bucking the group was primarily an emotional decision. But each time a subject went along with the group's incorrect answer, activity increased in the part of the brain dedicated to vision and spatial perception. In other words, in response to group pressure, the subject's *perception* of the shapes changed. (*New York Times*, "What Other People Say May Change What You See," June 28, 2005.)

If other people's opinions can alter the way we perceive shapes on a computer screen, can they also affect the way we see the far murkier shape of our future? Such abstract phenomena haven't yet been studied in an MRI, but it's a good bet that they can be. So for safety's sake, be judicious about whom you talk to!

DREAM BIG BUT START SMALL:
MOVING FORWARD IN INCREMENTAL STEPS

Few people are able to leap whole hog into a new career. More often, the obligations and concerns we discussed above make the path slower and less direct than you'd like. But if you are patient and creative you *can* keep your career transition moving forward. If money, family, and other considerations require you to take an incremental approach, consider some of the following options.

Get a part-time job in your new field. Judy Bennett enjoyed her eleven years as an elementary school teacher, but somewhere along the line she began nursing the idea of moving to the hospitality industry. But with no background in sales or marketing, how could she make the switch? When she heard about a part-time job at the Sacramento Convention and Visitors Bureau being the registrar for major conventions, she applied and was hired. From those contacts she was asked to be part of the opening team for a floating hotel, the Riverboat Delta King, a restored historic riverboat docked in Old Sacramento. She was given the title Public Relations Manager and was put in charge of planning and implementing events, giving VIP tours, and handling the media. While at the Delta King, Judy met her mentor, a woman

> "I've surrounded myself more with artists and creative people. I seek out local people who do art. I go to gallery openings. I find artistic people who will keep me on task and feed my curiosity and artistic-ness. Professionally and socially I've created a whole new world for myself."
>
> *Paula Lewis, former pre-press artist at a print shop, now professional graffiti artist*

DEFINITELY NOT EASIER,
BUT WORTH THE TIME AND EFFORT

Linda Struthers, who started her floral company, Lulu Potts, after a long corporate career, now enjoys mentoring budding florists. Linda believes that the biggest challenge for would-be entrepreneurs is their tendency to romanticize their dream business. "They think, 'wow, I'll get to play with flowers!' but the truth is, it's very strenuous, physical work; you're on your feet all day, lifting heavy boxes of flowers and vases; then there is the requisite cleanup of the studio and washing buckets and vases. Once this is complete, there's the ad to write, a marketing piece to print, fielding the customers' calls, and finally, paying bills and studying your P&L to see if you are achieving your financial targets. They underestimate the range of skills needed and activities required to run even the smallest business." That sentiment—that the work of starting a business is far harder than expected—is echoed by most successful entrepreneurs. Here's a sampling:

"When I first started the business I thought, I can take vacation any time I want! Wrong! Don't assume it's going to be easier because you're working for yourself. You're not! You're working for a multitude of clients—for all the people who are allowing you to *think* you're working for yourself."

Louie Richmond, CEO, Richmond Public Relations

"It's a lot more work than I ever anticipated. I think of myself as a hard worker, and dedicated, but when you own your own business, every little thing is your responsibility."

Jessica Caulfield, owner, Jessie James, women's clothing boutique

"We have it all on the line. We used our savings for seed money and remortgaged the house two weeks after it was paid off. With George's job we have enough to pay off the home equity loan on the house, so if worse comes to worst, we might lose the business and the building but we won't lose the house. On the other side, we don't have to worry about spending money going out to eat or going on vacation because we're too busy working!"

Paul Holje, co-owner, Dakota Harvest Bakers

who was in the process of starting her own public relations agency. She decided that she, too, wanted to do PR, so she applied to the UC Davis extension program in public relations and marketing. When she completed the program she was hired to be the public and community relations manager for Del Webb Corporation, developer of retirement communities, to open its first nondesert Sun City in Roseville, California. "In my opinion," says Judy, "that was my lottery win. I've been with the company since 1994 and I still absolutely love my job." When Judy left teaching in 1986, she had no idea she'd end up at Del Webb, she just knew the general direction in which she was headed. But by being open to opportunities she was able to step her way closer and closer to the job that became her dream.

Do your dream job on the side while keeping your existing job. Mark Spoto and his wife mortgaged their house to finance Mark's Dunn Brothers Coffee franchise, but they couldn't forgo the income and benefits Mark earned at his software job. So he continued to work full-time and opened the coffee shop by working evenings and weekends. He expects to keep the software job for at least several more years. "My goal is to open several more shops," he says, "and until I do that I can't quit. I'll be working at the shops evenings and weekends. But that's okay. Relaxation to me is having a project to do on my day off."

Volunteer in your new field. Connie Hilliard knew as a teenager that she wanted to be a talent agent but when she sent her résumé to local Chicago talent agencies, she quickly learned that talent agent jobs were few and far between. She would need experience and contacts if she was going to realize that dream. So she decided to get inside the industry in whatever ways she could.

First, she enrolled at Columbia College, which had a degree program in music business management, the closest thing she could find locally to talent agenting. When it came time to do her internships, she did two, both in talent agencies, where she learned different aspects of the business. Next, she got a certificate in sports management at Loyola University, another cousin to her dream. But to her dismay, the schooling didn't land her a position in a talent agency, where it seemed that getting a job was as much a matter of whom you know as what you know. So after taking a job as a claims processor in an insurance company, Connie embarked on a program of volunteering her way into a talent agency position. She joined an association called Women In Film, which provided networking opportunities, and through the organization did a mentorship with a talent agent. She volunteered for a Warner Bros. distributor, helping him promote records. She worked with a professional musician helping her sell her CDs. And she volunteers at a public television station on weekends helping with their pledge drive. "People say I'm crazy to do my twenty million jobs." She laughs. "But I just keep doing them because one day I'm going to get there."

In fact, not long ago, she learned of a vacancy at a payroll service that processes payroll for talent. She applied and was hired. Now Connie processes payroll for Chicago-area talent agencies. Every day she talks on the phone with the people who are in a position to hire her as a talent agent.

Take a job that is a transition to your new career. Maria Costen found a job that was "the perfect stepping-stone" to her dream career. Although Maria had worked for many years in marketing and sales, her dream was to be the host of a travel television show. When she learned of the opportunity to vocation with Kate Rice, an on-air style host, she jumped. "Kate was great," Maria says, "because she brainstormed a process with me to get from where I am to where I want to go. Kate started out being a spokesperson for Mervyns and was able to parlay what she learned in her nine-to-five job into going off on her own. She helped me figure out the steps so I could do that too." Kate's advice was to get a job that combined her skill set and her passion. For Maria, that meant using her skills in advertising and marketing, and her passion for television and travel. With a little searching, she found a job that involved all four elements: doing sales for TurnHere Productions, a company that produces informational videos for distribution online. Half of the company's videos are hosted travelogues, exactly what Maria hopes to do, and Maria is now immersed both in selling those videos and in watching them get made. "Every day I see them do a travel show," she says. "I'm getting paid to learn." At the same time she is bolstering her on-air skills with classes at the Learning Annex and through Toast-masters so that she can take that next step into her dream job.

Pursue your dream job as a hobby until you are ready to change careers. Gerry Gherardini is a chemical engineer at a pharmaceutical company who also happens to love making wine. His first foray into wine making took place in the mid-1990s when he talked his way

IF YOU'RE STARTING A BUSINESS:
ADVICE FROM LOUIE RICHMOND

Louie Richmond, founder and CEO of Richmond Public Relations in Seattle, and a VocationVacations mentor, was a classical musician for twenty years before he talked his way into a job as the director of marketing, advertising, and public relations at the Alexis Hotel. Talk about a career switch! From the Alexis, Louie moved to the Sheraton, where he held a similar position for nine years, but even with a decade's worth of experience and over two dozen awards to his credit, he still had a lot to learn when it came to starting his own firm. Here are Louie's words of wisdom to people venturing out on their own.

1. *Be ready to get out of your comfort zone.* You're moving from an area in which you're successful to one where there's a lot you don't know. Give yourself time to learn the basics. You can not-know a lot and still have confidence that you can proceed.
2. *Get support from a spouse, partner, or friend.* You can't do this in a vacuum.
3. *Find a support mechanism in your new career.* Allow yourself to say, "I don't know, please help me." Find a group that can give you the help you need.
4. *Allow yourself to make mistakes* because no matter how old you are, or how bright you are, you will.
5. *Get a good lawyer, a good financial planner, and a CPA.* Without those three people on your team you won't be successful. A lawyer will stop you from making stupid mistakes. A financial planner will help you create a good 401(k) plan

for your staff. A CPA will make sure your books are accurate and legal. You wouldn't believe how many companies go out of business because they don't pay their taxes.

6. *Invest in technology.* When I started I got the cheapest phone system I could. It broke within a year. Believe you're going to have a future and be willing to invest in your own company.

7. *Get a line of credit for emergencies.* Customers don't always pay after thirty days but your staff and your landlord still need to get paid. Don't use your house as collateral if you can help it because if you lose the business, you lose the house.

8. *Don't work in your pajamas.* If you meet with customers, don't have your office in your house. Don't use Yahoo or Gmail for your company e-mail. It's an image thing. What image do you want to project to your customers? You have to live that image. Treat yourself like your own customer. Invest in professional-looking graphics and a professional-looking Web site. Whatever your business, give yourself the quality you want to give to others.

9. *Don't automatically assume you're going to take a salary.* I didn't for three years.

into a group of older Italian men in Chicago who made wine using traditional, old country methods, including scheduling activities according to the phases of the moon and adding very little to the grapes. Gerry found the process fun and the product delicious, but the chemist in him was unsatisfied. He wanted to experiment with ingredients and see what happened. So the following year Gerry and a friend invested in equipment, which they installed in Gerry's basement and garage; bought grapes from California; and made wine themselves. They experimented with the sugar and sulfite content and blended different varieties of grapes, and by the following spring when they turned out 300 bottles of wine, the two men were hooked. For the next decade they produced 300 to 450 bottles of wine a year.

But a part of Gerry was still unsatisfied. With his knowledge of chemistry, he knew there was more he could do to control the outcome of his product. How did commercial wineries develop recipes? And what was involved in running a winery? With a wife and two young children he was not about to leave the security of his job, but was running a winery something he might want to do in "retirement"? Two days of vocationing at an Oregon winery answered his questions. He learned that running a winery *was* as hard and financially challenging as he had imagined—but something he still wanted to consider for the future. And he acquired a chemist's insight into the wine-making process. By working closely with the professionals, he learned how to take his own wine making up several notches.

Today, Gerry's wine making is a far cry from the traditional old world methods he learned that first year. The equipment and protocols he uses are similar to ones he uses in his professional work, and the result is wine over which he and his partner have a great deal more control. They intend to continue making wine in the basement for many years. Perhaps one day, when his children are grown, he will trade in his chemistry lab for some rich soil and grapevines, but for now he has the best of both worlds: a secure job and a highly satisfying hobby.

DOUBLE THE TIME, DOUBLE THE MONEY

Regardless of how you plan to transition to your dream job, one of the biggest challenges is keeping your expectations realistic.

It's so easy to get carried away by your own enthusiasm, to believe the rest of the world will love your business as much as you do, or that your new employer will immediately see your value and give you as much control (and money) as you'd like. But in truth, things rarely turn out to be as rosy as you think they will—simply because so many factors other than your enthusiasm influence your rate of success. Consumer tastes, the state of the economy, unanticipated events, the performance of the company you've gone to work for: so many elements beyond your control can have an impact on your performance. That's why, whether you're going to work for someone else or starting your own business, you need to follow the career transition rule of thumb: *Double the time, double the money.*

Expect it to take twice as long to become successful as you think it will, and to cost twice what you expected to get there.

If you're starting a business from scratch, expect it to take twice as long as you initially projected to earn a profit, and expect to spend twice as much money as you projected before you turn a consistent profit.

You think you can turn a profit in a year and a half? Plan for it to take three. Line up financing that will carry you for three years and then close the loan early if your optimistic projection comes to pass. Undercapitalization is the number one cause of new business failures: by the time the owners realize they're in financial trouble, it's too late to salvage the company. Avoid that by planning from the beginning to need double the money.

If you're taking a job in an existing business that involves starting at the bottom or taking a pay cut, expect it to take twice as long as you imagined to get to the position and salary you ultimately want.

Do you think you can leave your current job, take a pay cut in your dream job, and recover your financial position within two

DON'T FORGO HEALTH INSURANCE

As you cut back on expenses to finance your transition, there's one thing you shouldn't cut: health insurance. If you live in the United States, medical costs can be very high and unpredictable. One unexpected hospitalization can wipe out all your business capital. So cut back in other areas and, at the very least, buy catastrophic health insurance which covers only major hospitalization. To do otherwise isn't being frugal; it's being foolhardy.

years? Plan on four—and budget for your transition accordingly. How will you cover your expenses in the meantime? Don't get caught by surprise when three years from now you love your work but can't afford to keep your job because you're simply running out of money.

Perhaps you've heard the old adage about traveling: pack half the clothes and twice the money. Well, it applies to career transitions too. Pack half the expectations (of rapid success) and twice the money, and you'll stand a much better chance of actually reaching your destination.

FEAR REDUX

One of the great benefits of doing a test-drive and stepping incrementally toward your dream job is that it makes the process far less scary than it would be if you made a wholesale change. But that's not to say it isn't scary. Change is change, and there aren't many of us who can take it on without missing a couple of heartbeats. Especially when it comes to committing ourselves financially. The moment of quitting the current job, or signing the bank loan, or plunking down your hard-earned cash is a stomach churner, no matter how carefully you've made your plan. Even people who the day before were certain they were making the right decision find themselves having second thoughts when it comes time to seal the deal.

That's when support is so essential. This is the time to call up that army of supporters you've acquired—your family, your friends, your cheerleader, your banker, your mentor, the experts who helped you make your plan—and ask each one (yet again!) to remind you why you're making the right decision.

It's also time to dig down into yourself and remember what this means at the deepest level: that you began this journey because you were unfulfilled, because important parts of you were buried, and that this is your chance to bring those parts to life. In truth, by the time you're committing money you've probably already passed the point of no return. Those parts of you that were dormant have already awakened and are probably unwilling to go back to sleep. So along with your fear, congratulate yourself. You're doing what most people never have the courage to do: step beyond the safe, the comfortable, the status quo and dare to live your dream.

7

WHEN THINGS DON'T GO ACCORDING TO PLAN

My "make a million" job with the dot-com back in Chicago never made me a million, nor did it last very long, but it did provide me with two invaluable assets. One was my boss and mentor, Nick Matic, who is still a great friend; the other was something Nick said to me one day. It was a terrible time: the dot-com industry was imploding all around us and we could feel the cold wind at the door. I'd just raced into his office spewing out some sky-is-falling information, but Nick looked at me calmly. "Who's having a heart attack?" he asked. "This is important, but how important is it on the scale of things that really matter?" I was so taken aback I actually stepped backward. Nick and I had talked a couple of times about the fact that we both had close relatives who had died early. It wasn't an idle question.

I think about that question now whenever I feel my heart rate tick up at some irksome challenge in the business. It's like a comma inserted into a sentence. It slows me down a notch, just enough to bring me back into control. And that's a lifesaver, because in VocationVacations, as in any business, challenges are a regular occurrence. In fact, if anything, dream jobs are more prone to challenges than ordinary jobs simply because they *are* our dreams. Our expectations are higher, making it easier to be disappointed, and our passion sometimes clouds our judgment, getting us into tricky situations.

In this chapter we'll look at some of the special hazards of having a dream career, as well as steps you can take to avoid them. We'll start with the challenges inherent in running your own business and follow with hazards that can occur when you work for someone else. And (following the lead of doctors, who always seem determined to test for the most dire illness first) we'll start with every dream job seeker's nightmare: the terror of losing it all.

THE *ABSOLUTE* IMPORTANCE OF HAVING AN *ABSOLUTE* FINANCIAL THRESHOLD

What is the single biggest factor that stops people from pursuing their dream jobs? I don't have to tell you. It's the terror of losing it all: the fear of giving the job a go and then ending up worse than you were before. Whether you are taking a pay cut in the job of your dreams, cashing in all your assets to start a business, or borrowing against your mortgage to go to school, the fear of losing everything is often the obstacle that sidelines the most wishful dreamer.

Indeed, those fears are very real; many of us have heard stories about people to whom that has happened. But here's the good news: that kind of loss is entirely avoidable. *Even if you are starting your own business, you need never be in a position to lose everything.* Many factors can cause a job or business to fail, including some beyond your control, but there is no reason for you to lose everything in the process. You can avoid that by establishing an *absolute financial threshold,* a financial point you will not go beyond.

* * *

When Lisa Lathrop and her husband Tim Perry opened the Wisconsin Cheesecakery they did everything right. Neither had ever started or owned a business (Lisa had worked in retail and hospitality and then for the state government, and Tim worked for a nonprofit that worked with at-risk teens), so they took SBA classes on how to start a business, read tons of books, and talked to numerous small business advisers. Tim kept his job so he could provide health insurance and pay the mortgage and Lisa continued to work part-time for the government for the first two years to supplement Tim's income. They did everything right—until they applied for a loan.

It was December 2001, just after 9/11, and everywhere they went, lenders and alternative lenders said the same thing: "There's no money available for small, food industry start-ups. You need to borrow against your credit cards or from family and friends. The only way you'll get a loan is to sign a personal guarantee." Lisa and Tim were shocked. They knew it was foolish to max out their credit cards, they were unwilling to ask friends and family to share their risk, and they had deliberately incorporated the business in order to shield their personal finances. But now bankers were telling them they had no choice but to put their personal assets at risk! When they attempted to sign a lease for a kitchen they were told the same thing, and when they tried to lease equipment, they heard it yet again. Briefly, they considered finding a partner who would provide financing in exchange for a share of the business, but they were reluctant to give up any ownership or control. So finally, uncomfortable with the decision but seeing no other option, they signed many personal guarantees. In their own words, that was their big mistake.

For the next five years, Lisa and Tim struggled to make the business work. Their product—gourmet cheesecakes made with top-of-the-line, locally grown, organic ingredients—was superb, and local restaurants and event planners snapped them up. But the business had no storefront (Lisa baked in a rented commercial-grade kitchen), which limited the business's visibility, and the Web site, weddings, and regular stints at the farmers' market weren't enough to generate sufficient retail sales. As a result, the retail side of the business never matched projections. Meanwhile, the costs of running the business grew. The small loan they'd gotten had gone toward building out the kitchen, and without access to another loan, they were forced to use their own cash. They exhausted their savings, borrowed on their credit cards, and then plowed through Lisa's retirement savings. Although their business plan had showed her drawing a salary, the money was never there; instead, Lisa worked eighteen-hour days, baking, supervising, delivering, marketing, and bookkeeping—all without pay.

In 2006, they realized they were in serious trouble. The business was still gobbling money and they had no more to give. They needed to do what they had resisted at the beginning, look for an investor. They put out feelers, looking for a silent partner who would contribute cash without demanding a say in the operation, but a six-month search failed to produce one. So finally, just before the holidays—before customers started placing orders that they knew they couldn't fill—they announced that they were closing.

The next several months were excruciating. They had lost the dream and Lisa felt like a failure. Almost worse, however, were the legal and financial ramifications of closing the business. Lisa and Tim were able to pay off most of their business creditors, especially the small companies that needed those payments to pay their own bills, but some large creditors went upaid and filed liens against their personal assets. As a result, in addition to losing their savings and retirement, and racking up extensive credit card debt, Tim and Lisa were now in danger of losing their house. With the advice of their lawyer they filed for personal bankruptcy.

Bankruptcy is a lengthy process and it will be several months before they know the full extent of their losses. Financially, at forty-five and forty-seven, they are essentially starting over. Tim still has his job and Lisa is working several part-time jobs; for the next several years they will be working to start over financially. For Lisa, especially, this is a period of transition, a time to make sense of what she has been through and to catch her breath before she thinks about what's next. Despite the loss, she is glad they opened the business. "If we hadn't done it I would always have wondered," she says. "In the end, what we lost is just money but what we have is priceless: the memories, the experience, the knowledge we gained. And we still have each other, we have our health, we have the things that matter. I loved doing it, even all those long days, and I would do it all again; but next time I would do it differently. You need to know the financial needs of your start-up and find ways to finance it before you start. And I would never sign personal guarantees. At the time we thought, either we do this or we close, and we weren't ready to lose the business, but next time I would turn the money down rather than sign personal guarantees. You have to be realistic about how much you're willing to personally put at risk. Next time I would get outside funding."

Lisa is absolutely right. In hindsight, she and Tim learned the two most critical lessons for protecting yourself from financial disaster when you create a dream business:

1. Establish an absolute bottom line, a financial threshold you won't go beyond; and
2. Before you reach that threshold, find outside money.

They weren't wrong to use personal savings. They weren't wrong to use their retirement. They weren't even wrong to use their credit cards or part of the equity in their home. Where they went wrong was in using *all* those assets, because by using all their assets they left themselves with nothing. Had they picked one or two assets as their bottom line and taken them off the table, they would still have those assets today.

(I should insert here as a caveat that my "take" on financing a business is a little riskier than some people's. Many financial planners advise against using anything other than savings. Suze Orman, for example, says borrowing against your house, tapping your retirement, and using credit cards are all bad ideas. Her advice: save money and work a second job until you've amassed enough to live on while you launch and grow the business. My own experience, however, as well as that of other entrepreneurs I know, is that starting a business on savings alone is simply not practical. It almost always requires a larger infusion of cash. Which leads me to *my* business financing method of choice: tap your other assets but do it "safely" by taking at least one of them off the table.)

How could Lisa and Tim have kept one or more of their assets off the table when lenders and suppliers insisted they sign personal guarantees? *By rejecting the offers of those vendors and instead finding outside investors.* Of course venders and lenders wanted personal guarantees: their own business model requires them to recover the money they lend. If the borrower defaults, the lender needs to tap the borrower's assets to recoup his loss. Investors, on the other hand, don't have that constraint. They are prepared to lose the money they invest because in exchange for their greater risk, they hope to get a significantly greater return. They would not have required a personal guarantee.

Tim and Lisa understood that and did look for investors, but by the time they looked, it was too late. Investors were probably out there: if a business is viable there are always people willing to bet on its success. But finding the right ones can take months or even years. It's a process that must be started long before the need is urgent.

Bringing On a Partner

Many people starting their own businesses resist the idea of investors. They're concerned that bringing on a partner will mean losing control, and they're unwilling to give up any ownership of their dream. But as Lisa and Tim found, it's often impossible to go it alone; for financial reasons a partnership may be unavoidable. Taking on a partner need not mean giving up control, however. You can bring on a silent partner who, in exchange for reduced liability, will stay removed from management and operations, leaving you in full control. Or, you can bring on an active partner whose skills and knowledge will augment your own, further strengthening the business. True, you'll no longer reap all the business's profits—but, then, neither will you hold all the risk.

One of our vocationers said to me as she was taking on a partner, "Google's founders only own a portion of their company (now that they've gone public). Wouldn't you like to own a portion of Google?" I had to agree. I'll take 15 percent of a $50 million dollar company over 100 percent of a $2 million dollar company any day!

If you need an investor in your company, first decide what kind of partner you want: an active partner who will take part in management and operations and whose skills will supplement your own, or a silent partner who will invest cash but, in exchange for limited liability, remain aloof from management and operations. Then, to find a partner:

- *Network.* The best way to find a partner or an investor is through networking. Talk to people inside and outside of your industry. Join trade groups and entrepreneurial organizations. Go to industry conferences. Talk to small business advisers, lawyers, and accountants who may know people looking for investment opportunities. And, yes, talk to your friends, family, and cheerleaders. Even if you're not taking money directly from them, you never know whom they may know.
- *Be specific.* Clearly outline all the terms of your partnership. Use lawyers and accountants to help you think through all the details. Discuss "what if" scenarios; for example: what if one of us needs to get our money out? What if one of us becomes disabled? What if one of us seriously disagrees with a key business decision?
- *Date before you marry.* Do a project together that requires problem solving, decision making, and meeting a deadline. Watch for red flags. Only "get engaged" if it feels as good in your heart as it looks on paper.
- *Ask tough questions.* Fully vet your prospective partner. Talk to his past partners as well as his lawyer and accountant, and have your own business advisers, employees, and other partners (if you have any) kick his tires. (Just be careful not to kick something else.)

If after a thorough search you can't find an investor, ask yourself tough questions. The people with money are probably seeing a problem with your business model that you are too close to see. Is the business not really as viable as you thought? Have you made serious miscalculations? Ask investors who have spurned you to tell you their reasons and then take those reasons seriously. It may be some of the best advice you'll get.

SOMETIMES YOU JUST GET LUCKY

In 1999 Valerie Agosta became a private eye. She had fantasized about being a detective since childhood—ever since reading her first Nancy Drew book—but it took a diagnosis of breast cancer and her sister's suggestion that she find something to occupy her mind and time to make her realize her dream. She already ran a small company called Death by Murder, which arranged interactive murder mystery games for parties and conferences. Now she paid $12 for a private investigator's license and opened a second company, Hanady Investigations, named for a firm in the Nancy Drew series. But opening a firm was one thing; doing detective work was another. How exactly did one become a private eye?

With lots of book knowledge but no practical experience, Valerie decided to pursue on-the-job training. She applied for a job she saw advertised in the local paper, investigating insurance fraud, and for the next year, trained by her new employer, she practiced the basic skills of investigation: surveillance, interviewing, and interpreting data. At the same time, she passed out business cards to everyone she met. "It's amazing how many people have something they want investigated," she says. Simply through word of mouth, she built up a sizeable clientele. One year after starting the insurance job, she left the company to focus on her own business.

From the beginning, Valerie had thought of Hanady as a partnership between herself and her sister. It was possible to do the work herself, but doing it with a partner made it much more fun. And, indeed, during that first year, the two sisters had a blast ferreting out information about errant wives and husbands, deadbeat dads and long-lost friends. Since both women were middle-aged mothers working part-time, they called themselves the Spy Moms, and soon local media began picking up the story of these two most-unlikely private eyes. But then, toward the end of the first year, Valerie's sister also developed breast cancer and decided to leave the business. Valerie, whose own cancer had gone into remission, was left doing the investigations on her own.

For the next three years, Valerie ran the business single-handedly. Most of the time the workload was reasonable, and whenever a media outlet requested an interview, she would get her sister to go along so there would still be two Spy Moms to match the business's image. But it was a lot less fun doing the work by herself and in the back of her mind she thought repeatedly about finding another partner. Somehow, though, she never made that happen.

Then, in response to a pitch that Valerie had sent them, the *Today Show* decided to do a Spy Moms story. Valerie was ecstatic. National television! A story that could generate national clients! She called her sister, brimming with the news, but her sister's reaction set her back: there was no way, she said, that she could do the show; she simply felt too ill. Valerie was chagrined. Here she had the PR opportunity of a lifetime—and no other Spy Mom to do it with her! For the next few days she prayed and puzzled over what to do. What she really wanted was a partner, a second Spy Mom with whom she could share the laughs and stresses of being a private eye. But there was no way she could find one in the few weeks before the show. The best she could do would be to find a person to *pretend* to be her partner. Then somehow she could find a real partner later on.

Ten days before the *Today Show* taping Valerie attended a

Death by Murder audition where actors were trying out for roles in a mystery game. Her attention was caught by a middle-aged actress named Mollie. When Valerie introduced herself, Mollie exclaimed, "I read about you in the paper! I've been wanting to find you but I didn't know how!" Almost before she knew what she was doing, Valerie blurted out, "I have to do a *Today Show* taping in a week. Will you be the other Spy Mom?" It was crazy, she knew, to offer that role to a total stranger, but there it was, out of her mouth—and it felt *right*.

Ten days later she and Mollie did the taping—and by that time Valerie knew that she had found her perfect partner. Mollie was outgoing and enthusiastic, compassionate about people's problems, and naturally intuitive at thinking through the cases. Just as important, she and Mollie were becoming close friends.

A short time later, Mollie joined the business. That was four years ago, and ever since, Hanady Investigations has had its full complement of Spy Moms. Together, she and Valerie make the most of their "middle aged mom" personas—pretending to videotape each other while really taping the people they're surveilling, striking up conversations with subjects who would never suspect them of being private eyes, dressing up in costumes when they feel it will increase their "credibility" with suspects. Above all, they have fun. "That probably wasn't the 'proper' way to pick a partner," says Valerie, "but it worked. This is a match made in Heaven. If we stopped the business today, we would still be best friends."

DO YOU KNOW YOUR *BUSINESS* AS WELL AS YOUR *PASSION*?

Having a firm financial threshold is essential if you don't want to lose all your assets, but, of course, the best way to avoid losing assets is to keep your business running smoothly. And that means avoiding the hazards that are inherent in running a business that is also your passion. One of those is confusing your love for the work with your knowledge about running a business. It's not uncommon for people to get into a career because it's their dream and only later, when it starts to founder, realize that they were ill-prepared for the *business*.

Linda Struthers was indignant when her accountant asked her if Lulu Potts, her garden pots and floral design company, was a business or a hobby. She had been running it for three years, had a steady stream of customers, and had poured thousands of dollars of personal savings into it. Of course it was a business! But as she and the accountant looked closely at her financial records, she realized that the accountant was right. Her business practices and operating methods were undisciplined enough that they obscured the truth: the business was not making a profit. Linda had casually established a net financial target she wanted to make every year but she had never devised an actionable plan for how to get there. As a result, while the home-based enterprise required little capital outlay and enabled her to write off a portion of routine expenses such as car payments, certain household expenses, and health insurance, financially it contributed little else. Linda had worked in the corporate world for twenty-five years; she had attended business seminars and heard the icons of business speak; but when it came to her own business, she had allowed her passion for the creative work to direct her activities and had temporarily "forgotten" all the excellent business knowledge she had acquired. Somehow her own business—grown from her love of working in the garden—had seemed like a different kind of enterprise. Now, incensed by her accountant's question, she realized that for all her love of the business, for all her hopes that it would grow and support her, she had never really taken it seriously. She had, in fact, treated it like a hobby.

Why had she been so willing to toss her business knowledge aside? When she probed deeply she knew the answer: it was fear of failure. The business was her passion and she desperately wanted it to succeed. If she took it seriously and it failed, the loss would be enormously hard to bear. But if she took it *half*-seriously and diluted her energies between the floral business and several other business interests and it failed, the failure would be more acceptable. This was all unconscious. Linda *thought* she was taking the business seriously, she thought she was doing everything she needed to do. It wasn't until her accountant pointed out her losses that she realized that in its current shape her business would not last.

With that awareness Linda threw herself into gear. She switched from a personal finance to a business bookkeeping software program and, with her accountant's help, set up a financial recordkeeping system that gave her clear measures of the business's income and expenses. She revived the annual financial goal she had set initially and determined how many products she would need to sell each year to make the target. She rethought her company's image: she had done all of her graphics work herself in order to save money, but now realized that if she wanted to appeal to a high-end market, she needed to look like a high-end business. So she hired a graphic artist and Web designer who produced classy marketing and collateral pieces. And with help from a business-savvy friend, she took a hard look at the profit margins of her two products and realized that the garden pots would never make her money. At that point she had to make a tough decision. She had started the business because she loved designing and planting garden pots; working with fresh flowers had been an after-thought based on customer requests. But now it was clear that fresh flower arrangements were where her profits lay. Faced with abandoning the business or retooling it for profit, she gradually phased out the garden pot business. Interestingly, as she turned her energies to learning the floral trade, she discovered that she genuinely loved working with fresh flowers. They required less physical labor than the pots, took up less storage space at her studio, and made purchasing supplies far simpler. And because she specialized in flowers for weddings and special occasions, the work enabled her to participate in the most celebratory events.

Once she had narrowed the focus of the company, Linda could invest her time and money more effectively. Her marketing became targeted because she now had one product to sell and could easily determine the number of floral events she needed to do to make her financial target every year. She no longer needed employees to help create the labor intensive garden pots, so she was able to eliminate her payroll. By focusing her time and energy, she was able to "look up from the workbench" and manage all aspects of the business. In short, she was able to be strategic rather than getting mired in operational details.

Looking back now at her early years, Linda could see that treating the business as a hobby had had costs she hadn't seen. She'd lost sales because her marketing efforts had been diluted and confused as she spread them between the pots and flowers; she'd lost income by focusing on an unprofitable product; she'd even lost money by trying to save money. Thinking she was being financially prudent, she had done her own bookkeeping with inadequate tools and knowledge, she had designed and printed her own logo and marketing materials, and she had relied on her own instincts to learn the floral trade when attending classes taught by professionals would have substantially shortened her learning curve.

"It's amazing how naive you can be, even when you've had the best training in the world," Linda says. "I was far too tolerant of doing less profitable business because I loved doing the garden pots and flowers. But you can't live on intangible rewards."

PASSION *AND* BUSINESS

Before you undertake your dream business:

- Make sure you know *all* aspects of the business, not just the part you love.
- Bring in experts to help with the parts you're not strong in.
- Avoid the "hobby trap" by:
  - *suspending disbelief that your business can be big and serious.* Think BIG and let that infect everything you do. If you can't summon that belief yourself, bring in advisers who can help you expand your thinking.
  - *making a business plan that projects growth.* If you don't plan *how* you'll reach your targets, you never will.
  - *asking for help.* Form a "board of advisers" with no fiduciary or legal responsibility but with various areas of expertise who can ask tough questions and give sound advice about every area of your business. They may enjoy meeting each other as much as they enjoy helping you, but a nice dinner would be a way of paying them for their time and advice.

IS THAT A *BUSINESS* DECISION OR A *PASSION* DECISION?

If you've ever spent a ridiculous amount of money on something you fell in love with but couldn't really afford, you know how easy it is to have your financial sense overruled by your passion. And that creates another challenge for dream business entrepreneurs.

Greg Hancock had been running his dream business very success-fully for three years when he let his enthusiasm lead him astray.

In 2000, at the age of thirty, Greg was getting ready to "retire" from AOL. He'd accumulated a decent nest egg and was ready to do something new, so when he and his wife fell in love with the town of Show Low, Arizona, 190 miles from their home in Tucson, he quit his job and they moved. They figured Show Low would be a good place to raise their children, and they could live off their savings while Greg figured out what to do next. What they didn't anticipate was the major downturn of the stock market. Within ninety days they lost almost all of their money.

Show Low, unfortunately, for all its charm, was not a place with high-paying jobs, so Greg took a job in a print shop for $9 an hour. Between the rental of their Tucson house and the remain-der of their savings, they managed to make ends meet, but Greg had other ideas. Before they left Tucson he had dabbled with an online business selling Apple computers and telescopes. Now, in the evenings, he started another online store. This one was dedi-cated to selling space-related paraphernalia and toys, and fairly quickly, working three to four hours a night, Greg began to turn a profit. By two years later he was able to quit the print shop; Space-toys was paying the bills.

For the next year the business grew. Greg, working solo, bought and stocked the merchandise and shipped it out, and his profits climbed steadily. But he was dissatisfied. His first love was tele-scopes and he missed the days in Tucson when he could hang out in the astronomy store near his house talking shop with other amateur astronomers. He wanted some way to do that again. And if possible, he wanted to incorporate it into his business. His ear-lier effort to sell telescopes online had fizzled, in part because the manufacturers supported only brick and mortar stores, so it didn't make sense to try that again. But what if he started a brick and mortar store of his own? That would provide the hands-on socializing he was missing, and it would be a natural addition to Spacetoys.

He was mulling that idea when a storefront opened in a Show Low mall. It didn't take long to convince himself he needed to take it: the visibility would bring in business, he'd get the social networking he craved, and Spacetoys would have room to grow because he could handle larger inventory.

Almost as quickly as he'd made his decision, it became clear that having the store was a mistake. Customers came in to talk, just as Greg had hoped they would, but they took enormous amounts of time and got in the way of sales. And while he was working in the store, he couldn't handle the online business—which meant that he was losing sales simply by standing in the store and talking to "customers"! At the same time, his overhead had skyrocketed. Now for the first time the business had rent, utilities, and employees. The former low-expense, high-profit business had become a cash-guzzling burden.

To solve the problem, Greg moved to a bigger store. A larger, less expensive space opened in a better location and he decided that more inventory and greater exposure would translate into greater sales. But instead, sales remained flat. The rent and utility bills and payroll expenses added up as the expanded inventory sat unsold in the cavernous space. Then a severe rainstorm flooded the store and Greg lost $2,000 in inventory. That was the sign he couldn't ignore: he moved Spacetoys back home. Unable to break the lease, he had to continue paying rent, but the savings—in payroll, utilities, and emotional strain—justified the expense. The entire experiment, which had lasted a year and a half, had cost him $21,000.

Ironically, as mistaken as the storefront venture was, it proved useful in the long run. When the business moved back home, its expanded inventory overran the house, so six months later the

MAKE DECISIONS WITH
YOUR HEART . . . *AND* YOUR HEAD!

Greg's decision to take on the storefronts so he could pursue his love of telescopes is just one example of how dream business owners can find their good judgment overruled by their passion. It's equally easy to overestimate the market for your product or service because you assume customers will love it as much as you do. *Or* to misread data and see what you want to see in the numbers. *Or* to believe that a change here, a change there will make an ailing business turn around even when the objective signs say otherwise. To avoid these mistakes, *have all your major decisions vetted by your cheerleaders and "board of advisers."* Take their advice seriously even if it's not what you want to hear.

Hancocks refinanced their house and built an office-warehouse on their property. Now, with a payment one-third the storefront's rent, Greg has a secure location with enough space to let his inventory grow. With no unnecessary expenses, most revenue drops to the bottom line. The business has become profitable enough that he has been able to hire employees and step back a bit from day-to-day operations. "Without that mistake I wouldn't be where I am today," says Greg. "But no question it was costly at the time."

WHEN THE JOB IS A DREAM BUT
THE COMPANY OR ORGANIZATION ISN'T

People who start their own businesses are not the only ones to face the "passion vs. objectivity" challenge. Vocationers who take dream jobs inside organizations may also face passion-related hurdles. It may be hard, for instance, to work with colleagues who are less devoted to the work than you are, or colleagues who have different ideas about how things should be done. Work conditions that in any other job might be perfectly acceptable may drive you to distraction because now your expectations are higher. Simply because it *is* your dream, and because you've taken a risk to pursue it, you have more on the line, yet there is much you don't control. What happens if the organization you work for gets in the way of the dream?

Many years ago I took a job at a company where the owner had a reputation for some rather ruthless behavior. I knew that. I had researched the company in trade publications and talked to people in the industry and had heard the whole story before I went in, but I believed that I could operate autonomously enough that his reputation wouldn't hinder me. By and large I was right. From time to time, a potential customer would ask who owned the company and then grow chilly when I told him. In those cases I knew immediately I would never get the sale. But for the most part, my boss's reputation had minimal impact on me.

I was fortunate. I wanted that job but it wasn't my dream and I was clearheaded enough to be able to examine the situation objectively. But one of the dangers of taking a dream job in an organization is that in our eagerness to take the job, we fail to investigate the situation fully. Or we do due diligence but then don't act on what we learn. As a result, we find ourselves in a situation that is not to our liking.

If you're taking a dream job in a company or organization, avoid that pitfall by reminding yourself that the job you get is only as good as the company you keep. A bad boss or a bad environment can turn your dream into a nightmare. Protect yourself from that scenario by doing the following:

- Talk to people on the "inside," if possible, about what the organization is like to work for.
- Investigate the company's reputation.
- Research the organization online: Is it in solid financial shape? Is it well respected? Have there been any lawsuits against the company or its leaders?
- Ask about your boss's management style: Does it mesh with the way you like to be managed? Do his employees regularly advance? Does he give adequate praise, support, and credit? Is he flexible? Will you have as much responsibility and authority as you want?
- Ask *business*people whose opinions you respect to review and evaluate your findings. Talk with them about the pros and cons of taking the job. In your eagerness to follow your dream, you may be apt to downplay anything negative but they can be objective. Listen to their advice!

Of course, passing your due diligence doesn't mean that a company or organization is perfect. Sometimes you get inside and discover that things still aren't what you wanted. Here, too, it can be hard to be objective when the job is your dream. Are the problems so severe, for instance, that you need to leave—or are they tolerable because you're doing what you love? Are you stomaching a bad situation because it really might improve—or because the job is supposed to be your dream? Are adjustments possible that would make the situation better?

Peter Zimmerman (a pseudonym) took a job with a nonprofit organization that served stroke patients and their families, believing it would be his dream job, and it was—*after* he tweaked it a bit to make it better meet his own personal mission.

After many years in academia, Peter was thrilled to land the job of program director at the organization. Both of his parents

EXPAND THE JOB TO MATCH YOUR PASSION

If it turns out your dream job description doesn't entirely match your passion, can you:

- create ways to do your "dream work" within the confines of the job?
- negotiate an expanded job description with your boss, perhaps over a specified period of time?
- use the platform of the job to do your "dream work" on the side, knowing that the opportunities you create now may lead to a better dream job in the future?
- use your insider's contacts to find a better dream job in a different organization?

had suffered strokes and he wanted to devote the rest of his life to reducing other people's risk of having one. But he had been in the job for only a few months when he encountered a frustration. The programs he felt were most important were not the ones the organization was prepared to deliver. While he perceived a tremendous need to educate the public about *preventing* strokes, the organization was focused on serving patients and families who had already suffered one. Peter understood that with finite resources the organization was limited in what it could achieve, but he couldn't help but think that it was missing a critical piece of the agenda. For a few weeks he dwelled on his frustration—then he took matters into his own hands. If he couldn't provide prevention programs *directly,* he would find ways to do them *indirectly* within the parameters of his job.

From that point on he looked for opportunities to get out the prevention message. Building on his credibility as program director at the organization, he approached the local university extension school about teaching a class on preserving brain health as we age. The university agreed, and the class became one of their regular offerings. He started an internship program at the organization for university students in the health and social services fields, in which the students learned not only about working with patients and their families, but also about prevention strategies that they could later disseminate in their own careers. He creatively pursued opportunities to appear in the media, pitching stories to both local and national outlets. And he expanded the content of his community presentations to include both risk factors and prevention.

Now, five years into his new career, Peter feels tremendously fulfilled. His first responsibility is always to stroke patients and their families, but by working creatively in and around that function, he engineers countless opportunities to engage the area that is his passion. Rather than dwell on the limitations of the job, he has used the platform of the job to do what he really wants to do.

WHEN THE CULTURE CLASHES

Glenn Goldman had a different kind of adjustment to make when he took a dream job inside an organization. For him, it was not an issue of mission, but rather one of culture.

Glenn's first love was aviation. From the time he was a child growing up on Long Island, planes were "in his blood." So it was not terribly surprising when after college, using money he had expected to spend on law school, he found himself taking flying lessons instead.

CULTURE SHIFT

Every career has its own culture, so any time you switch to a new line of work you're apt to find yourself in a semi-foreign land. You may find new ways of thinking, new vocabulary, new supervision styles, new sacred cows . . . In addition to learning the ins and outs of the new job, you need to adjust to new ways of thinking, acting, and working. If the culture at your dream job feels awkward initially,

- *give it a little time:* there are probably so many new things hitting you all at once, you need to give yourself time to adjust.
- *find a translator:* find someone who is familiar with the culture you've come from as well as the new one and ask him for feedback. His perspective may help you through the transition.
- *look for the good:* instead of dwelling on the things you don't like or the things you miss, look for the positive elements in the new culture. If you can stay open-minded, you may discover new opportunities to grow.
- *take the long view:* remember that you took this job because you love the work. Can you look beyond the culture shift to the work itself and stay connected to your passion?

Within a year he was teaching at the school where he had taken lessons, and within another year, he and a friend had bought a small flying school of their own. He was living out a dream.

In the back of his mind, though, was the shadow of another dream: being a commercial airline pilot. Flying "heavy metal" would be a lot of fun and pilots made good money; part of him wanted to move in that direction. What held him back was the regimented lifestyle. In his current job he worked when he wanted and had time to pursue other interests. At an airline he'd be a prisoner of the airline's schedule. So each time the shadow dream surfaced he brushed it aside and stayed with what he was doing.

By the time he and his partner had owned the flight school for five years, however, Glenn felt himself getting restless. The challenge was gone from teaching and he was ready for a change; he needed to grow or switch careers. Was this the time to become a commercial pilot? Still uncertain, he applied to several airlines, and when none of them responded, he took their silence as a sign: he was meant to give up aviation. So he sold his half of the business, pulled up stakes, and moved from New York to Montana, where, in the shadow of the Rockies, he decided to pursue another long-held dream. He enrolled in graduate school and got a master's degree in counseling psychology.

For the next nine years Glenn worked as a therapist in Missoula and Seattle. He loved it. He loved working intimately with clients and colleagues; loved the deep, probing conversations; loved the warm, embracing culture. But as he approached forty, he began to have second thoughts. The increasing emphasis by insurance companies on "brief therapy" and medication was pushing therapy in a direction he didn't believe in, and while he had managed to save a little money toward retirement he wasn't where he wanted to be. The future was looking less than rosy. So he began once again to consider his options. And the more he thought, the more he knew what he wanted to do. He wanted to return to the dream that he'd sidestepped ten years earlier.

So in 2000, at the age of forty, Glenn updated his aviation credentials and applied to Horizon Air. The airline told him to get some light plane experience and then come back, and when he did, he was hired. He has been there, happily, ever since.

But the change did not come without challenges. Interestingly, the challenge he anticipated—the degree of regimentation—was not as difficult as he'd expected. What did take adjusting to, though, was the airline culture. The sometimes macho attitudes of the pilots could not have been more different from the emotional embrace of the therapy community and Glenn missed the deep, personal conversations. He worried that he wouldn't fit in, that he would never be "one of the guys." For his first few years at the airline he wondered if he had made the wrong choice.

With time, however, those concerns began to fade. He began to make friends within the pilot community, and within the cockpit itself he experienced rewarding camaraderie and teamwork. And while flying didn't permit him to work with people on their deepest issues, it did challenge him to think in new and different ways. Instead of engaging the emotional side of his brain, it demanded a linear, analytic way of thinking that he found satisfying. Seven years into his new career, Glenn now feels comfortably at home. Once he stopped needing the culture to be like the one he was used to, he was able to find much in the new culture to enjoy.

WHEN THE JOB CEASES TO BE A DREAM

Peter Zimmerman and Glenn Goldman are lucky: they've been able to work around their frustrations without compromising their dreams. But not everyone is so fortunate. Sometimes the frustrations that come with a dream job are simply too much to bear. Sometimes the only recourse is to leave. For Pat Tryon (a pseudonym), the very qualities that make her job a dream job also make it time for her to leave.

Pat is associate athletic director at a well-respected university. Her job is to administer the university's varsity sports program, which includes supervising coaches, negotiating contracts, handling NCAA compliance, managing tournaments, and interacting with students. She has been doing it for thirteen years and it is absolutely her dream job, the job she worked toward from the time she graduated from college. But it has also taken over her life to the point where she feels chronically exhausted and resentful. Although the duties of the job are the ones she wants to perform, the hours have made the job untenable. "I still love it," she says. "There are days that are very rewarding. But I'm worn out: it's not a job, it's a lifestyle. I work almost every weekend, I can't even have a dog because I travel so much, and I have so little free time that I don't even know what to do with it when I have it."

Throughout her twenties and thirties, Pat regularly worked sixty hours a week but it didn't seem problematic. Most of her colleagues did the same, she loved the work, and having grown up in a culture that valued hard effort, she expected to perform at that level. But as she approached forty, her feelings began to change. She began to notice that her life was out of balance. When a friend expressed surprise that her boss had called her on a Sunday while she was on vacation, she realized he was right, and when her parents said, "You shouldn't be so tired that you have to sleep all weekend when you finally have a weekend off," she knew that they were right as well. She found there was an emptiness at the center of her life—that friends, family, and outside interests had all been pushed aside to make room for the job—and she didn't want to live that way anymore.

But it was too late to make a change. The culture of the industry simply didn't allow it. "This is the way it is in collegiate sports,"

WORK-LIFE BALANCE

The biggest reason we pursue our dream jobs is to increase our life satisfaction. We're willing to work hard—we may even relish working hard—because we believe in what we do, but we also want to be able to put the work aside and enjoy the other aspects of our lives. We want our dream jobs to feed us, not deplete us.

Most dream jobs require extra work at the beginning. Whether you're new in an organization or getting a business off the ground, you often need to put in long hours until the job becomes stable. But you put in those hours expecting the start-up period to be finite, expecting that after the initial tidal wave you will find the proper balance.

Unfortunately, it's easy to get caught up in the undertow and not notice how long that "new job" period is lasting. Loving the work, wanting to succeed, you fail to notice how demanding the job has become, or how much of a toll it has taken on the rest of your life. You don't notice until the job has stopped feeling like a dream.

Help yourself keep your job a dream by instituting safety measures that let you track and evaluate your work-life balance:

- *Do a semiannual "lifestyle checkup":* Write down a description of your dream lifestyle. Every six months take it out and measure your current life against it. Are you moving toward it? If not, what action steps will you take *before* your next checkup to keep yourself on track?
- *Create a Board of Lifestyle Advisers:* Ask two or three people whose opinions you trust to meet with you after each semiannual checkup. Ask them to keep you on track by monitoring your action steps and asking hard questions.

she says. "I could rattle off the names of twenty other women who have the same title and the same personal issues." In a sense, Pat is a captive of her dream. The very qualities that drew her to her job and enabled her to succeed—her passion, competitiveness, and drive—are the same qualities that are causing her burnout.

Did it have to be this way? Not necessarily. Pat thinks it might have been different if she had seen the writing on the wall and taken action earlier. "I should have listened to other people who said, 'The way you're working isn't normal,' back when I was younger," she says. "I should have started carving out better control back then. If you work sixty-plus hours a week when you're in your twenties and thirties, that's what people expect of you. Maybe I wouldn't be here if I hadn't done that."

But she did do it, and now she *is* here, and she is trying to take charge of the situation. The NCAA has created a committee on work-life balance, but its efforts are unlikely to produce any rapid, significant changes, so she is starting to think about changing careers. She is setting aside money to help with a transition and thinking about what else she might like to do. Her experience in this job—with its tremendous upside as well as down—has taught her a great deal about what she does and doesn't want. She has a lot of information to work with as she identifies her next dream.

TURNING IT AROUND

If dream jobs sometimes offer greater challenges than ordinary jobs, they also offer greater second chances. The incentive to overcome a hurdle, or turn a bad situation around, is all the greater because it's driven by your passion. That's why it's not unusual to see vocationers bounce back just when you thought they were down for the count. Jan Townsend did that when her first dream job failed. She took everything she'd learned, revised her dream career, and relaunched it to great success.

For Jan, 2001 was a really tough year. Her marriage ended, she moved to a town where she knew no one, September 11 shook the world, and then she was diagnosed with colon cancer. She was fifty-eight years old, the life she had known was gone, and as far as she could see, there was absolutely nothing to replace it. Fortunately, her new home came with wonderful new neighbors. Sharon and Doug "adopted" Jan; they had her for dinner several nights a week and nursed her through her despair. They were there as Jan slowly started to think about what she wanted to do with the rest of her life. The synchrony of the divorce, the cancer, and the devastation of September 11 had convinced her that she wanted to go somewhere in the world where she could make a difference, so when Sharon introduced her to a friend who was doing volunteer work in Guatemala, it felt like a match made in heaven. Within months, the two women went together to Guatemala, where they volunteered in orphanages and on coffee plantations, and a few months later they formed a nonprofit organization. Their plan was to raise money from North American foundations, coordinate with Guatemalan social service agencies, and then to make extended trips to Guatemala to implement the funded service projects. Jan's spirits soared. For the first time in a year she felt she had purpose in her life. Her depression lifted, her energy returned. She threw herself into the work.

By the women's second trip, however, things began to unravel. When Jan made suggestions, her partner rejected them. When their visions of the organization clashed, the woman overrode her. As they put together their business plan, the partner insisted on doing it her way. More and more Jan became the literally "silent" partner because nothing she had to offer was accepted.

Nine months into the partnership she realized there was no way they could work together.

Jan broke off the relationship and then went into a tailspin. She had wanted so much for it to work; the project had imbued her life with meaning and direction and now that was all gone. She felt as if she had failed. The depression of the year before returned and for six months she wondered how she would survive.

To Jan's continual surprise, however, people who knew about her work in Guatemala kept asking her to speak. Church groups, women's groups, and library groups all wanted to hear about her Guatemalan projects. At first she resisted; her partner's criticisms had shaken her confidence and she didn't feel up to the task. But little by little, she responded to the invitations. And each time she spoke, she remembered the deep connection she had felt with the Guatemalan people and the feelings of purpose, joy, and satisfaction she had felt when she was there. She realized she had to find a way to continue the work.

But something else became clear as well: she didn't want to do it alone. The profound connection she'd felt with the Mayan people was something she wanted to share. The proper vehicle for her, she realized, was not a partnership in which she and her partner would do all the work, but an organization that enlisted many people in working side by side with their Mayan hosts. Jan began researching volunteer projects in Guatemala and found Helps International, an organization that combats Guatemala's high rate of lung disease and childhood burns by sending volunteers to replace families' traditional indoor fire pits with efficient wood-burning stoves. She e-mailed for information, and when the organization encouraged her to bring a group of volunteers, she recruited eleven people, mostly from her church, to go.

The rest, as they say, was history. "Once my mind was made up

BOUNCED!

Back in 1978, my brother Terry and his wife, Kathy, decided to start a Barefoot Grass lawn care franchise. They went to the bank and took out a $5,000 line of credit using as collateral a small inheritance left by Kathy's dad. The bank put the cash into a checking account in the business's name and Terry and Kathy started spending it—on office furniture, equipment, a bulk mail permit . . . the things they needed to get the business running. Imagine their surprise when one by one, the vendors started calling, claiming their checks had bounced. How could that be? Terry called the bank and after a little detective work it turned out that the bank had inadvertently deposited the money into the wrong account! The Barefoot Grass account was empty. The bank corrected the error and Terry made them write a letter of apology to all the vendors—but it was a heck of a way to start a new business.

and I made that first connection with Helps International," Jan says, "things just fell into place. It was like it was meant to be." More groups invited her to speak, and friends told friends, and she had no trouble filling more trips. Soon she had formed a nonprofit organization, the Hearts and Hands Foundation, and was taking groups of twenty-five to Guatemala three or four times a year. With each traveler paying his or her own way, plus buying one or more stoves for installation, the organization was self-supporting. She added an educational component, teaching four "in-services" at the beginning of each trip, about Guatemalan history and culture, and added a week of cultural tourism at the back end so that clients would come away with an understanding of the country and the people.

With additional trips and travelers, the foundation's projects were able to expand. By its second year, foundation volunteers were installing water filters in homes, bringing doctors and dentists into remote Mayan villages, building kitchens in schools where 70 percent of the children were malnourished, paying teachers' salaries, and funding scholarships for girls who could not otherwise go to school. Soon, Jan hopes, they'll be able to build a medical clinic. But as important as these achievements are, they are only part of what Jan feels is the foundation's larger mission: promoting intercultural understanding. "My big goal," she says, "is to have people from different worlds learn about and accept each other. I want to be a drop in the bucket to achieve world peace."

Just two years after her first venture fell apart, Jan is achieving that goal. She is quick to credit the times ("since 9/11 people want to give back to the world in some way"), but her success is equally a testament to her own fortitude and vision. She has what most vocationers have, the quality that sets them apart from those who wish for dream jobs but don't take action. She has *resilience*. She foundered when her first venture fell apart but she didn't stay down for long. She revised her project and found a different way to make it work. She didn't take no for an answer.

That ability to rise again is common among vocationers. Many call themselves "stubborn" (as do people who know them) and attribute their success to their ability to persevere. "The only thing that kept us going was my bullheadedness," I've heard more than one vocationer say. But their "bullheadedness" is of a particular kind. It's not the stubborn refusal to admit defeat or to see things from a different point of view (although many vocationers do that too). Rather, it's the deep-seated belief that they will succeed—if not now, in this venture, then in the next. It is an attitude about life as well as work, a belief that we can make our lives the way we want rather than conforming ourselves to an ill-fitting box. That, more than anything else, is what distinguishes a vocationer from other people. Vocationers may find that in the dream job world things don't always go according to plan—but more often than not, they hatch their next plan pretty quickly.

8

HAPPY VOCATIONING!

As a teenager, Jerry Vandiver wasn't adept at sports and he didn't care about cars, but when he heard a group of kids at his church camp singing songs and playing guitars, he knew he was hooked. Back home, he got on a bus to downtown Kansas City, bought a used guitar and a songbook, and started taking lessons. From there, it was only a matter of time before he started writing his own songs. By the age of fifteen, Jerry had found his identity.

After college, Jerry went on the road, playing venues from music clubs to Holiday Inns and "singing 'Mr. Bojangles' in more bars than I want to remember." After a while, however, the traveling life grew old, as did the meager living. So he dusted off his college biology degree and went to work as a seventh grade science teacher. The work was good—he liked the kids, he liked the financial stability—but he couldn't bring himself to stop performing and writing songs. Even on school nights he'd stay out doing gigs till 1:00 or 2:00 in the morning. The performing was a necessity. It kept him in touch with his dream.

One night, while sitting in a bar waiting to go on, he watched Barbara Mandrell's show on TV. It would be so cool if one day she would record one of my songs, he thought. He had no inkling that, years later, she would.

A few years into teaching, Jerry decided to visit Nashville. He didn't imagine moving there, or pursuing songwriting as a career, but he wanted to size himself up against the competition. The trip was fun—he met with a few songwriters and publishers and got the lay of the land—and he returned to Kansas City unchanged. But then he went to Nashville again . . . and yet again. When he returned from Nashville the fourth time, a fellow teacher looked him in the eye and said, "You're going to do it, aren't you?" It was exactly the prod he needed to admit to himself that he was. Ten months later he made the move.

In Jerry's first five years in Nashville, he drove tour buses and worked weekends to pay the bills, and gave most of his time to writing songs and doing the enormous amount of networking that was required to get them heard. There are believed to be between twenty thousand and forty thousand hopeful songwriters in Nashville, so the competition was fierce, and the music business was a revolving door. No sooner had he made the acquaintance of one producer (or the producer's receptionist), than that person would leave and he'd have to start relationship building all over again. Just pitching his songs felt like a 24/7 business.

Then there was the learning curve. Jerry had come to Nashville feeling he was a decent songwriter—but now he found himself in a place where the bar was really high. The only way to stay in the game was to continually "up" himself, to try to make each song better than the last. But the stiff competition also meant that he was going to "grad school" in a city full of teachers. Everywhere he went—clubs, bars, meetings with other writers—there were musicians he could learn from. All he had to do was keep his mind and his ears open.

When Jerry had been in Nashville for almost five years he got his first song recorded. It was "Don't Waste It on the Blues," sung by country music star Gene Watson. To his utter amazement it hit number five on the country charts. If Jerry hadn't been in Nashville long enough to know better, he would have thought that his career was made: a publishing contract, performers clamoring for his songs, one hit rolling out after another. But he did know better: he knew there were tons of writers who were one- or two-hit wonders, and that having one hit song was no guarantee he would even get another one sold. So when the thrill of having a song at the top of the charts began to wane and he could concentrate again, he went back to the guitar and the pad of paper, and started writing more songs. "In this business, you're only as good as your next hit," he says. "I just had to take a deep breath and try to prove myself again. I'd have to do that every day."

That next hit did not come quickly. Despite the fact that he was writing every day and pitching songs continuously, it was a year before he had another song recorded and on the charts, and that was when Wild Rose recorded his song "Go Down Swingin'" and took it to number twenty. That success felt as good as gold—but still, it didn't come with a guarantee.

So over the next seven years, Jerry continued to write and pitch and learn. And more than for most of the hopeful songwriters in Nashville, his talent and industry paid off. His songs were recorded by country greats Lee Greenwood, The Oak Ridge Boys, Latin great David Lee Garza, as well as Dusty Drake, Phil Vassar, Lonestar, and a then not-so-well-known artist named Tim McGraw, who recorded Jerry's "It Doesn't Get Any Countrier Than This" on Tim's *Not a Moment Too Soon* CD, which has gone on to sell over six million records and was awarded the ACM (Academy of Country Music) Album of the Year award. His song "For a Little While," sung by Tim McGraw, soared to the top of the country charts and was performed on the David Letterman show. The CD was awarded the CMA (Country Music Association) Album of the Year award and "For a Little While" subsequently found its place on Tim's *Greatest Hits* CD.

The success was fantastic—but still the pitching and learning didn't stop. Even with his songs appearing on over fourteen million records, even with an ASCAP and a BMI award and two record titles on the wall at the Country Music Hall of Fame, Jerry was still only as good as his next title. Lean years, with income in the low five figures, were followed by six-figure years, which were followed by the occasional year in which his income never even broke $1,000. Wisely, Jerry had invested in real estate and rental properties, which meant that even in "bad" years he could make ends meet without taking another job. But he could never let up. "There's never a resting place," he says. "There's always room to improve, always someone new to meet and network with. The only difference now is that, most of the time, they'll take my call!"

Today, Jerry is widely recognized in the country music business not only for his songs, but also for his generosity and ability as a teacher. He teaches workshops through numerous professional songwriters' associations, and mentors children and adults who want to learn the art and craft of songwriting. It's his way of acknowledging the songwriters who came before him and who helped him succeed. That he has succeeded so handsomely still astonishes him. He works now in a little home office where the platinum CDs of his songs by Barbara Mandrell and Tim MGraw hang on the wall. "I never thought it would be this good," he says. "I've answered my wildest dreams. I still want to write the CMA [Country Music Association] song of the year, I still want to win an Oscar. But I've already reached my biggest dreams. Now I can just let my imagination get even wilder."

* * *

What Jerry's story illustrates so clearly is that having a dream job is a journey as much as a destination. Yes, you've arrived at the work you love, but the work isn't static—it's constantly demanding more—and you have to continually rise to the challenge if you want to succeed. You have to learn new skills, improve your old ones, push yourself beyond assumed limits. No resting on your laurels here. That's one of the pleasures of a dream job: it forces us to grow.

And dream jobs don't just force us to grow professionally; they propel us to grow as people. They push us to face our fears and find our way past them; to examine our values and stand up for what we believe; to confront habits or attitudes that are no longer functional and decide to move on.

Dream jobs take us out of our comfort zones. They push us into the *discomfort* zone, which is where all growth happens, and force us to try new behaviors, find new strengths, and see ourselves in new ways. As Lea Chadwell said about her gradual transition from veterinary technician to baker, "I'm doing things that, for me, are not the norm. Learning the science of baking, taking time off from work, asking to change my work schedule: those are things I would have avoided in the past. But now, because I really want to make this change, I can do them."

SATISFACTION

Back when Doug and I were driving across the country and I was doing my non-scientific market "research" for VocationVacations, I asked people what kinds of jobs they dreamed about. But what I got back from them wasn't just a list of job titles. What I got was a list of job *qualities*. People wanted to feel passion for their work, they wanted a sense of purpose, they wanted to feel that the work they did *mattered*. They also wanted a sense of constructive challenge. People didn't describe a life in which they spent eight hours a day in an easy chair; they wanted to engage in activities in which they could learn and grow.

I immediately thought back to those conversations when I read about the work of Dr. Gregory Berns, the Emory University neuroscientist I've quoted in earlier chapters, and my first introduction to his work was his book called *Satisfaction: The Science of Finding True Fulfillment*. In it, Berns describes humans' seemingly insatiable quest for satisfaction, profiling a diverse cross-section of people from ultra-marathoners to practitioners of S&M, who go to extremes to find it.

Satisfaction, according to Berns, is not the same as pleasure or happiness. Rather, it is a state of contentment, enlightenment, tranquillity, and sensing something beyond our own existence. It "captures the uniquely human need to impart meaning to one's activities." I read that description and thought *yes!* That's exactly what vocationers are looking for. That's exactly what we want in our dream jobs. I kept on reading—and then Dr. Berns's research got *really* interesting. What brings us satisfaction, he believes, is not simply *having* the thing or experience that we believe we want, but the *challenge* of going after it. It is in the quest for satisfaction that we find it.

Berns backs up this statement with biology. Using functional MRI technology, he observed subjects' brains as they tackled challenges and reported on what they were feeling. When he and his colleagues studied the MRIs, they discovered that the interaction of two hormones, dopamine and cortisol, seemed to produce the feelings we associate with satisfaction. That dopamine was involved was not surprising: dopamine is the hormone secreted in the brain in anticipation of pleasure. But the presence of cortisol was unexpected. Cortisol is the chemical released when we are under stress. Why would a stress chemical be present in the brain when we are feeling satisfaction? Berns hypothesizes that it is the element of challenge combined with the anticipation of meeting that challenge that produces the sense of satisfaction. Or said another way, it is "the tension between what is predictable and safe versus what is novel and dangerous."

I read that explanation and thought how aptly it described the process of switching to, and continuing to build, a dream career. Over and over in that process, we feel the anxiety of moving forward into the "novel and dangerous" world of our dreams, *and* anticipate the pride and pleasure we will feel when we are able to navigate there safely. Vocationing is a continuous, rising cycle of challenges and resolutions, the perfect combination of stress and pleasure. No wonder people are driven to pursue their dream jobs! No wonder we continue to feel satisfied in our dream jobs even when the work is hard and the hours are long and the money is uncertain! We may lack sleep, we may lack vacations, we may lack financial security, but all the while we are mixing that potent cortisol-dopamine cocktail. At the emotional and biological level, we feel fulfilled.

I realized, when I read about Berns's research, that I was wrong when I was researching VocationVacations. It's not simply the jobs that people find so rewarding. It's not simply the hands in the dirt, or in the cookie dough, or on the grapevines. It is the continuing opportunities to stretch and learn, and then to revel in our growth, that make us so passionate about our vocations. It is the continuing challenges that make working at a dream job so satisfying.

GROWING THE BUSINESS, UPPING THE CHALLENGE

The fact that we find pleasure in our challenges also makes us restless in our jobs. You might think that after a challenging first year learning the ropes of a new career, we would take a breather when things start to feel more comfortable. But in the world of dream jobs, that rarely happens. More often, when vocationers feel their learning curve lessen, they look for the next challenge. That inner drive that compels us to learn and grow pushes us to take our jobs to the next level. Dawn Casale, whom you read about in Chapter 6, has done exactly that with One Girl Cookies. She has grown the business in a series of stair steps, engaging and solving one challenge at a time.

Dawn began the business with a mission: to provide beautiful, and beautifully packaged, gourmet cookies. After testing recipes on family and friends, she settled on the several cookies that would be her staples and began baking and packaging them in her tiny New York City apartment. She sold them over the phone: after years of working in New York, she thought she knew enough contacts to build a successful business filling private orders. Within six months she realized she was mistaken. Her Rolodex of contacts wasn't enough to support her and she needed additional customers. How would she find them? By wholesaling: selling cookies in bulk to other businesses. What businesses might want her cookies? Caterers. She pulled out the yellow pages and started making calls. To her delight, several caterers agreed to include her cookies in their menus. Next she called Dean & Deluca, one of the country's premier gourmet markets. The Manhattan store agreed to carry the cookies and also to let her come in and give out samples. It was a marketer's dream: a gold-plated opportunity to meet her target customer face-to-face. Between Dean & Deluca and the growing list of caterers, her revenues grew.

But she was selling only in New York City. From Dawn's earliest days she'd imagined having a national mail-order business. If she could find a way to package the cookies so they wouldn't break, she could greatly enlarge her market. How to do that? She began to experiment. One Girl's signature boxes—wrapped with decorative paper and featuring old sepia photos of her family—weren't sturdy enough for shipping, but if she added a protective layer inside . . . She tried various forms of packaging until she found a layered system that kept both the boxes and the cookies intact. Then she was ready to pursue national mail order. She sent samples to national food and bridal magazines, and the gorgeous packaging combined with the unusual product caught editors' eyes. Little photo features appeared in several magazines and national mail orders took off.

By March 2002, almost two years into the business, demand had outgrown the capacity of Dawn's apartment. The obvious solution was to rent a commercial kitchen, but she knew that would radically change the business. From the beginning, her only significant expense had been payroll—a full-time baker and a part-time packer-delivery person. With a kitchen she would add rent and utilities to the mix; the financial pressure would become enormous. But it was a move she knew she needed to make. So she rented a kitchen and redoubled her efforts to find wholesale customers. Gradually, she brought new ones on.

Then a customer unwittingly introduced her to another revenue stream. The woman asked if Dawn sold cookies packaged as wedding favors. That idea had never occurred to Dawn, but instantly she saw an opportunity. "Yes!" she answered, and within a week she had created a set of beautiful, individual cookie packages, each one customized with decorations and a message reflecting the bride and groom. Dawn added event packaging to her line of products and the favors quickly became popular with caterers and brides for bridal showers and weddings. By the following November she had enough business to hire another baker.

For the next three years business remained stable, ramping up at the holidays, then dropping down to "normal" the rest of the year. But even as it settled into a pattern, it was growing in Dawn's mind. She knew the business was limited by its lack of a storefront. Without a street presence, it lacked visibility and therefore sales; and while media coverage, which she depended on to drive retail customers, had been good, it would be far better if she had a photo-friendly destination. So in 2005 she and Dave Crofton (who had come on as a baker back in 2002 and since become her husband) leased a storefront in the vibrant Cobble Hill section of Brooklyn and opened One Girl Cookies, the shop.

Once again, the business changed. Expenses tripled; the staff tripled; the physical plant introduced a whole new set of challenges. In retrospect, the financial pressure created by the move to the kitchen seemed like a minor inconvenience. But there were tremendous upsides to the change as well. For the first time, Dawn and Dave weren't limited to products that were suitable for shipping, so the product line expanded. Customers became regulars, forming a committed relationship with the brand. Revenue increased and retail sales began gaining on the wholesale side of the business. By the end of the first year, the shop had not yet broken even, but it was clear to Dawn and Dave that it was headed toward profitability.

Dawn and Dave are now finishing up their second year in the shop. Business continues to grow and, of course, with the growth come yet new challenges. How can they continue to increase production of their handmade baked goods while also keeping labor costs relatively stable? How can they produce lines of custom cookies for commercial accounts without disrupting their own production schedule? How can they satisfy their bakers' needs for change and creativity while also meeting customers' demands for regular items? These are tricky questions with no easy answers— but these days, what gets Dawn and Dave excited about going to work every morning is the puzzle and anticipation of finding solutions. At the same time that they tackle these operational issues, they are also considering their next *big* career move: opening a second store. They figure a second location is still two years away, but it's not too soon to start the planning. Their drive to grow—not just as a business, but as individuals—demands it.

TIME TO MOVE ON

There may come a time, however, when even a dream job becomes less satisfying—a time when the learning curve flattens and the challenges subside. A time when you find yourself fantasizing about something new. Seth Godin, author of many books about business, says that many people—even happily employed ones—stay in their jobs too long. They stay past the point when they've grown comfortable. My own theory is that people who work their dream jobs actually reach this stage faster than other people because the same qualities that push us to realize our dreams also make it imperative for us to move on. Once the learning stops, we get bored. We start looking for the next challenge.

If there's anything that holds a vocationer back from moving on, it's apt to be a sentimental attachment to the job. You've put so much of yourself into this career, how can you leave it behind? You've labeled this career as your deep-held dream; how can you turn away? What will friends and family think if you do? The answer is: *we change.* What we love in our twenties may be wholly different from what turns us on in our thirties, and what fills us with passion in our forties may be different from what gratifies us in our fifties. Thank goodness! Think how boring it would be if we always stayed the same. Nowhere is it written that you commit to a dream career for life. What *is* written is that you be true to yourself and follow your heart.

So if after some time in your dream career you find yourself losing steam, ask yourself these questions:

- Are there ways I can stretch my job to make it new?
- Can I move to a more challenging job in the same field?
- Can I take my business or organization to the next level?
- Or have I wrung as much challenge and satisfaction from this career as I need to?

Talk to your advisers and others in your industry and see if they have ideas for how you can wrest more growth from your job. And then, if you feel as if you've done everything you can, move on. Don't stay for the sake of staying. Don't settle for less than you want. After all, you've already found or created a dream job once. Who better than you to do it again?

THE TWENTY-YEAR VISION

It may seem odd to talk about the end of your dream job when you've only just begun to find one, but thinking that far out is actually an important part of the process. That's because creating a dream job isn't just about a job; it's about how you live your life. It's about the *attitude* with which you live it. Taking the steps to create a dream job means giving up the idea that you will conform your life to *other* people's dreams. It means making the decision to draw your own life map and steer yourself along it. It means creating a vision of the life you want to live and then actively moving yourself toward it. That isn't an attitude that most of us inherit. Generally, we're taught to take the safe route: to work a steady job, make a steady income, avoid unnecessary risk. Stepping outside the box is implicitly discouraged. But by

THE FIVE ATTRIBUTES OF
THE SUCCESSFUL VOCATIONER

1. *Optimism:* You believe you can do it. You know it's risky and there's a chance you'll fail, but in your gut you believe you'll succeed.
2. *Vision:* You know where you want to go.
3. *Confidence:* You know failure is survivable. You may lose time and money, but you will gain in knowledge, experience, and self-esteem.
4. *Determination:* You would rather try and fail than not do it. You don't want to wonder later, "what if?"
5. *External support:* You have the key people in your life behind you.

pursuing a dream job, you've rejected that way of thinking. You've already taken a step toward building the life you want. The next step is to create a long-term vision.

Two years before I actually started VocationVacations—somewhere between the time I thought of the name while sitting in traffic and the day I packed up my desk at the dot-com—I wrote down a long-term vision for the dream job lifestyle I knew I wanted. I still have the paper on which I wrote it. Here's some of what it says:

20 year vision

1. Be in a happy, loving, passionate, long-term relationship
2. Own my own VocationVacation-esque company (note the "esque" part: I wasn't sure yet what it would be)

3. Live a "grounded nomad" life, traveling between homes in desirable locations
4. Have my own TV show or special
5. Write a monthly or quarterly column in a national magazine or newspaper
6. Be on the *Today Show* and/or *Oprah*
7. Trek a major mountain
8. Go whitewater rafting
9. Travel to all 7 continents
10. Establish a scholarship fund in my parents' names

After I wrote the list, I placed it in the back of the leather work binder that fits snugly inside my laptop bag, and it's still with me wherever I go. It's tattered now and has coffee stains all over it. Few people ever see it. But I pull it out once a month or so to review it . . . envision . . . and dream. When I wrote it, those goals seemed pie-in-the-sky. I had no idea how I would achieve them; I just knew they were important. But now, just six years later, seven of the ten shown here have already come to fruition and the others are in the works. That's not because I'm luckier, or more capable, or even more driven than other people; it's just because I wrote them down. It's because I had a clear vision of what I wanted to achieve.

The power of visioning is remarkable. When we create a vision for our future, we lay down neural pathways in our brain, essentially blazing a path for our actions to follow. As writers and researchers in areas from sports to leadership have pointed out, "rehearsing" actions in our mind is one of the best ways to encourage peak performance—and it's as true in achieving life goals as it is in exceeding a quarterly sales goal or acing a serve in tennis. When you clearly imagine your future, you make it easier for yourself to live it.

The key is to envision your future concretely—not with a hazy, feel-good picture, but with specific goals you'd like to achieve. Do you want to live in Europe? Start a business? Own horses? Be home when the kids get home from school? Each one of those needs to be part of your vision. Do you want to work from a

> "As a businessperson, if you're not changing and growing, you're dying."
>
> *Duncan Goodall, owner,*
> *Koffee on Audubon*

sunlit office with a fabulous view? Put that on the list. The more concrete and specific you make your list, the more of it you'll achieve. There's nothing mystical here; envisioning things doesn't somehow "will" the universe to provide them. The "magic" is simply that taking time to define your goals and write them down points you in their direction. Hang-gliding teachers like to say, "Look at the blackberries, land in the blackberries," meaning, whatever you focus your gaze on is the way you'll steer. And that's exactly how it is in life. Whatever you set your sights on is what you'll direct yourself toward.

Most people set their sights on the ordinary because that's what they've been conditioned to expect. But you've already decided to move beyond that: you're pursuing a dream career! Now go ahead and flesh out that vision. Go online, research your career, and imagine *yourself* in those online photos. Then imagine the life that goes along with them. Where will you live? How will you spend your days? What will you do when you aren't working? Imagine yourself as a mentor and picture someone coming to *you* for a vocation!

Chances are, you've been thinking about this change for a while. How much longer are you willing to wait? *This* is the time to create your dream career and lifestyle.

Test-drive your dream. Take the steps to make that lifestyle real.

Go out and do it.

Happy Vocationing!